Welcome

Few products have captured the public imagination like the iPad. It looks so simple – just a thin slab of metal and glass – that you wonder what could possibly make it so special.

And then you get your hands on one...

If this is your second or third iPad then you know exactly what we're talking about, and if you've used an iPhone or iPod touch, you'll have some inkling. If you're just setting off on the road of iPad ownership, though, you have some wonderful treats in store.

It is the iPad's legendary simplicity that lies at the very heart of the tablet's success. Aside from topping up the battery, you need never attach it to anything. No USB ports, no memory card slots, no upgrade options... You buy it, you use it, and you enjoy it; as simple as that.

You don't need to think about configuration, operating system options or diagnosing faults. All of its software is thoroughly vetted by Apple to ensure a smooth and trouble-free experience, and there are no viruses, Even the physical hardware design is a work of true engineering genius.

Combined, these factors have helped power the iPad to the number one spot in the market. No other tablet sells in greater number, and no other tablet is served by as wide a choice of applications as the iPad through its dedicated online store.

So, what's not to like?

Well, perhaps one thing: no matter how deep you dig through the smart cardboard box in which it arrives, you won't find much of a manual.

That's where we come in.

The Independent Guide to the new iPad is your end-to-end handbook for choosing and using Apple's miraculous slate computer. We'll help you pick the model that best suits your needs and, when you've got it home, set up your email, parental controls and security options to keep it secure and help you retrieve it should you ever misplace it.

More than that, though, we'll also introduce you to some of the iPad's most exciting applications. We'll show you how to edit your pictures in iPhoto, assemble a video in iMovie, put together a killer presentation in Keynote and produce great-looking letters in Pages. We'll work through a budget in Numbers, show how to compose your own song – without any musical experience – using GarageBand, and use the core iOS apps to keep in touch with friends, enjoy music, books, and even get travel directions to wherever you need to go.

The iPad is a remarkable, versatile gadget that one day we will look back upon as an era-defining product. It marks the point at which we stopped thinking of computers as heavy, cumbersome objects that sat on our desks, or at best our laps, and became properly wireless, portable, carry-anywhere devices. It's no exaggeration to compare it to the switch from landlines with rotary dials to mobiles.

This is just the beginning...

Welcome to the future.

Nik Rawlinson

The Independent Guide to

The new iPad

....

WRITTEN BY Nik Rawlinson

ADVERTISING
MAGBOOK ACCOUNT MANAGER Katie Wood 07971 937162
SENIOR MAGBOOK EXECUTIVE Matt Wakefield 020 7907 6617
DIGITAL PRODUCTION MANAGER Nicky Baker 020 8907 6056

DENNIS PUBLISHING LTD
GROUP MANAGING DIRECTOR Ian Westwood
MANAGING DIRECTOR John Garewal
MD OF ADVERTISING Julian Lloyd-Evans
NEWSTRADE DIRECTOR David Barker
CHIEF FINANCIAL OFFICER Brett Reynolds
GROUP FINANCE DIRECTOR Ian Leggett
CHIEF EXECUTIVE James Tye
CHAIRMAN Felix Dennis

PUBLISHING AND MARKETING
MAGBOOK PUBLISHER Dharmesh Mistry 020 7907 6100
MARKETING EXECUTIVE Paul Goodhead 020 7907 6012

LICENSING AND REPRINTS
Material in *The Independent Guide to the new iPad* may not be reproduced in any form
without the publisher's written permission. It is available for licensing overseas.
For details about licensing, contact Carlotta Serantoni, +44 (0) 20 7907 6550, *carlotta_serantoni@dennis.co.uk*
To syndicate this content, contact Anj Dosaj-Halai, +44 (2)20 7907 6132, *anj_dosaj-halai@dennis.co.uk*

Contents

Chapter 1: Welcome to the iPad

YOUR CHOICE!
Alternatives to iTunes and the iBookstore
p64

Chapter 2: iPad applications

Turn the page for even more...

Watch us **You Tube**
Like us **f**
Follow us **t**

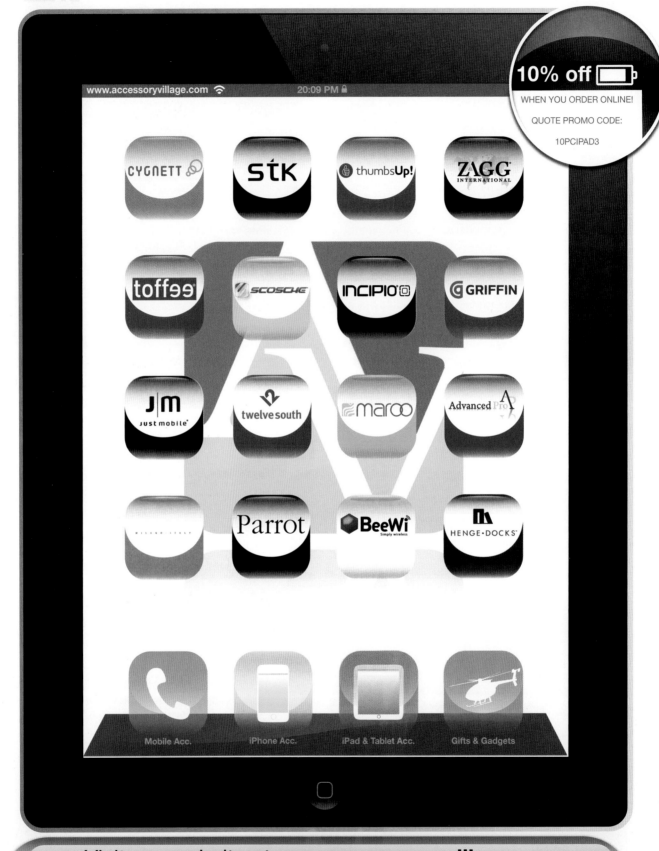

www.accessoryvillage.com 20:09 PM

10% off
WHEN YOU ORDER ONLINE!
QUOTE PROMO CODE:
10PCIPAD3

CYGNETT · STK · thumbsUp! · ZAGG INTERNATIONAL

toffee · SCOSCHE · INCIPIO · GRIFFIN

J|m JUST MOBILE · twelve south · maroo · Advanced Pro

Parrot · BeeWi Simply wireless · HENGE·DOCKS

Mobile Acc.   iPhone Acc.   iPad & Tablet Acc.   Gifts & Gadgets

Visit our website at **www.accessoryvillage.com**

Cases & Covers, Chargers, Batteries, Holders, Car Kits, Handfree, Bluetooth Accessories, Docks, Screen Protectors,
Speakers, Headphones, Data Cables, Styluses, iPhone Accessories, iPad Accessories, Tablet Accessories,
Kindle Accessories, PC Accessories, Apple Accessories, Gifts & Gadgets

All major credit cards accepted

Chapter 3: How to...

The Independent Guide to the new iPad

Chapter 1
Welcome to the iPad

What is the new iPad?

You've no doubt seen an iPad – at least in pictures if not in real life – but what lurks behind that smart, bright, touch-sensitive screen? Here are the key features of the new iPad and how it differs from its predecessors.

The iPad is perhaps the most remarkable product that Apple has ever produced. Even the original iPhone, which was a revolutionary device leaps and bounds ahead of the competition at that time, would have trouble coming close.

Perhaps only the original Mac, released to almost universal acclaim back in 1984, could be said to have ever come close. That machine completely re-thought the idea of personal computing, incorporating many high-end ideas that previously cost several thousands dollars to buy – such as the mouse and graphical interface – into in a machine that, while not 'cheap' wasn't so far out of the reach of the average consumer or everyday business user. In many respects it, too, 'changed' computing.

Although Apple has had many great successes since then, including the transparent iMac that relaunched the company following Steve Jobs' return, and the iPod with

which it reinvented the idea of portable, carry-anywhere, personal music players, only the iPad comes close to emulating what the company achieved with the first Macintosh. Now in its third iteration as the 'new' iPad, the device has slowly and logically evolved, retaining its initial appearance (more or less) but upgrading the screen and processor.

The iPad and iPhone may both run the same operating system and share many apps from the integrated App Store, but it's only when you get your hands on an iPad, with its larger screen and all of the functionality it enables, that you truly appreciate what a remarkable device the world's first mass-appeal tablet really is.

It's at that point that you understand why Apple now espouses a concept of living in a 'post-PC' era, at the heart of which sits the iPad. By this it means simply that we've moved beyond the point where we need to think in

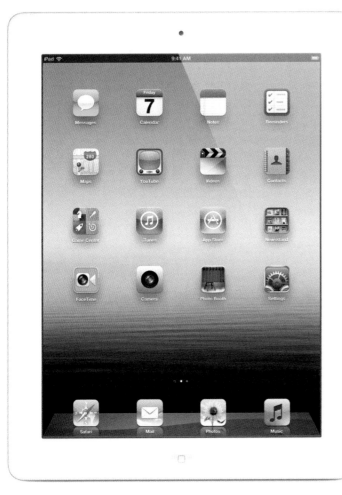

terms of keyboards and mice, specs and performance data. Instead we need to think only about our documents, photos and music files – in short, what we *make* and *do* with our device. We don't even need to think about where they are stored, but instead simply get on with using them, on whichever device we happen to be holding.

Life in the cloud

In Apple's eyes we are no longer tied to a desk and a conventional computer; all we want to do is access our data from the cloud, wherever we happen to be, whenever we need it, and on whichever device we happen to have on us at that time.

It would make sense, therefore, if we thought of the iPad as a window into the world of work and play. While we may create original page layouts, photomontages and cinematic videos on our Macs and PCs, it's getting ever more likely that we will want to access an increasing

amount of our content via a tablet device. It just so happens that Apple has the best tablet on the market. Why, then, would we choose to use an alternative?

But it goes beyond content consumption: we can also use our iPad to create original content.

Courtesy of iMovie we have a full-blown video editing application; iPhoto is a first-class photo organisation and editing application; GarageBand lets us pull together studio quality music tracks; Quickoffice, a Microsoft Office-compatible productivity suite will handle our word processing, number crunching and presentation design. Countless magazine publishers have produced their own applications that allow us to consume the latest media without buying print-based products that will need recycling when we've finished reading them, and even broadcasters are getting into the act by coding tailored applications for accessing back-catalogues of their archived content.

Should we not therefore also be talking about a post-TV world, too? As the years go on, more of our time will be spent with a tablet in our hands, through which we'll experience a greater and greater portion of the world and in our daily lives. In the short term at least, the likelihood of that tablet being an iPad is very high.

So is Apple right? Are we indeed living in a post-PC era? Well, look at it this way... you can work for a whole day on the iPad without touching a traditional computer, and when you've finished you can use its built-in e-mail application to share the fruits of your labour with friends, family and colleagues. You can have video chats that will enable you to work remotely, access files on a shared server and chat using a host of mainstream messenger apps. You can catch up on missed TV and listen to international radio stations. You can take and edit your photos and movies...

All of these are tasks for which we would once have turned to our computers. In that respect, yes – we are indeed in the post-PC era. This is the age of the tablet. It's the age of the iPad.

The new iPad

The 'new' iPad is the tablet's third-generation iteration. Announced in San Francisco on 7 March 2012 by Apple CEO Tim Cook, it saw the company drop the version number of its predecessor, while the tablet itself gained a little weight and some attractive new features. It hit the shelves just 9 days later.

The physical differences between the latest iPad and its predecessor are so minor that unless you saw them side by side you would be hard pressed to tell them apart. Even comparing it to the original iPad shows how little the external appearance of Apple's tablet lineup has changed over the first two years of its existence.

Look closer, though, and you'll see that there are indeed some differences. While the iPad 2, which remains on sale, was lighter than its predecessor, the new iPad has in fact put on a little weight. It still boasts the gently curved sides and flat back

of the iPad 2, though, and again comes in two colours: black or white. Only the front is coloured; the back is aluminium in both cases, with a narrow strip of plastic on the 4G-enabled device. It's remarkably thin, and the 9.7in screen is the perfect size for tucking into a bag or carrying around without getting in the way, while still being large enough to use as a practical work monitor or interface for reading web pages and magazines.

On introducing the iPad 2 nine months earlier, Apple had done away with the old, clumsy fold over cover that enveloped the original iPad, and provided it with an effective support for typing, replacing it with what it called the Smart Cover (*see below*). These remain Apple's choice of case for the new iPad.

These neat, colourful covers are held in place by magnets that form a hinge on the left side of the iPad's body when held in portrait orientation. The covers themselves roll out of the way to form a triangular stand to support your iPad when typing, or lie flat across its back when you're holding it in the crook of your arm and tapping the screen. They have a flock-lined underside to protect and clean your screen when it's closed, and as the iPad can detect the cover's presence thanks to magnets in the opposite side, closing a Smart Cover puts the tablet to sleep, while opening it wakes it up.

Naturally, this feature interested developers, and the coders behind Evernote, the note-taking application, were quick to come up with Peek, a flashcard app that displays only part of each note when you lift the first section of the Smart Cover, and reveals the rest when you lift it completely. This allows you to, for example, view a foreign word in the first

quarter, and only see its definition when you've lifted the rest of the cover, having tried to recall for yourself the translation.

Under the hood

With the release of every new generation of iPad, Apple has steadily improved the tablet's underlying technology. Where the first iPad used an Apple-designed A4 processor (the first processor Apple had ever designed in-house), the second generation device moved on to use the A5. The new iPad upgrades this once again to the A5X. This can do everything the A5 did, but more quickly and with better features for handling graphics, thanks to a quad-core graphics processor built in.

This bolstered graphics-handling capability is an important point, and not just for gamers who will want a more responsive output, because the biggest differentiator of all between the new iPad and its predecessors is the resolution of the display. In the new iPad this has leapt from the conservative 1024 x 768 pixels of the iPad and iPad 2, to an enormous 2048 x 1536 pixels. To put this into context this is roughly the same number of pixels as you would have on a conventional 27in computer monitor. However, because they are squeezed into a 9.7in panel they are much more densely packed on the new iPad. This means that each one is too small to be seen by the human eye without some kind of magnification, even at very close quarters. Apple calls this screen technology Retina Display. If you think that sounds familiar, it is: it was first seen on the iPhone 4, and later the iPhone 4S. This display is without question the biggest selling point of the new iPad.

No wonder Apple called it 'resolutionary'. And no, that's not a typo.

As has always been the case, the iPad comes with a choice of three capacities: 16GB, 32GB and 64GB. Even the smallest of these is sufficient for hundreds of applications, e-mails, address book entries, music tracks and photos.

However, no aspect of any iPad is user upgradable, so unless you're prepared to dump what you already have and buy an entirely new device, you should think very carefully about how you'll use it and therefore which capacity you might need when choosing which to buy.

If you only plan on browsing the web and sending e-mails, then 16GB will be more than enough storage. If you'll be downloading music and synchronising videos with a Mac or PC, then you might want to consider 32GB. Even with double the capacity, though, most users will still have to be selective about the media they keep on their device and regularly swap tracks, movies and so on with a main library on their Mac or PC.

If you're an avid reader of magazines and plan on switching from print- to pixel-based publications, then you would be advised to opt for the largest capacity device so that you can keep a back catalogue of magazines with you. This does, however, contribute to a significantly higher price, so you need to judge how much that convenience is worth to you. It is undeniably cheaper to get into the habit of deleting magazines once you've read them, safe in the knowledge that you can usually download them again from the publisher should you need to refer to them in the future. This will allow you to buy an iPad with a smaller capacity at a lower price, leaving you a larger budget for buying media.

Communications

Every iPad has built-in wireless networking with which to connect to your home or office network, or access public networks in coffee shops, airports and other places where people congregate.

They also have Bluetooth connectivity, which allows you to hook up wireless speakers for streaming music, or use Apple's own wireless Bluetooth keyboard for typing. If you plan on using your iPad as a work device then it could well pay dividends to invest in a keyboard (and other manufacturers, including Microsoft are getting in on the act, too) as it will save you typing on the screen all the time. It's more comfortable, and because there is a degree of movement in the keys that isn't present when tapping directly on glass it will be easier on your fingers.

However, where external communications are concerned there remains a big difference between the two halves of the iPad lineup, with the more expensive devices also allowing for connections to the public cellphone network – for data transfer only.

The iPad and iPad 2 could connect at best to third-generation (3G) networks, as used by most smartphones. However, the new iPad is Apple's first 4G (or Long Term Evolution – LTE) device.

4G currently allows speeds of 100 megabits for so-called high-mobility communications, where the device accessing the network is travelling at high speed, such as in a car or train. At lower speeds or when static it should be able to achieve up to 1 gigabit per second of data throughput. Although this depends on network coverage, and 4G is not yet available worldwide (the UK doesn't have it yet), in those served areas such speeds significantly exceed those offered even by most wired consumer broadband services.

At the same time as receiving this bump to its data capabilities, the iPad has borrowed a neat trick from the iPhone. The new Personal Hotspot feature allows it to share its data connection with other wirelessly-enabled devices, so if you're using a regular wifi iPad and your friend has the 4G edition, you'll able to piggyback their public data connection to extend Internet access to your own device. Note, however, that in doing so you will eat into their own monthly data allocation.

Even if you don't think you'll need such high performance data connections when away from a regular wifi network there's another significant reason why you may want to consider the 4G-enabled iPad: GPS satellite navigation.

The mobile data chip built into the 4G-enabled device (and the 3G-enabled iPad 2 and iPhones from the iPhone 3 onwards) also contains the necessary hardware for accessing and decoding data from the GPS constellation. Originally a military tool, this is an arrangement of – currently – 31 orbiting satellites that send a time code to compatible receivers such as the iPad. These receivers compare each of the timecodes from all of the satellites from which they can receive a data stream and use this to triangulate their position. This allows them to accurately plot their current location on a map.

This is useful for refining the results in applications like Find my iPhone, which can locate a lost iPhone, iPod touch or iPad, and for enabling proper turn-by-turn navigation in route-planning apps.

Even if you only opt for the wifi-only iPad you'll still be able to find your current location as the iPad will look up your position with reference to your current network address. So long as you have a wifi connection it's surprisingly accurate, often getting to within a few feet of your current location. If you don't have coverage,

however, you'll obviously not be able to use this feature.

Cameras and photography

The second generation iPad was the first to introduce a front-mounted camera. This enabled both photography and video conferencing using the built-in FaceTime software, which is compatible with iPads, iPhones, iPod touches and the Mac, and thus meant that anyone who had bought into any part of Apple's system of computers and portable devices could chat to each other online for free. Although it wasn't the first company to do this – companies like Skype had been offering it for years – it was one of the simplest and thus most effective implementations.

It also had a rear-mounted camera at a higher resolution than the front one, which was used for taking photos. Each of these cameras remains in place on the new iPad, with the lower resolution front-mounted camera perfect for passing fairly conservative amounts of video data across your network to remote participants in a video call, and the rear-mounted camera more suited to stills photography and shooting video footage at full high-definition resolutions (1080p) at 30 frames per second with audio. The results of this are perfect for use in apps like iMovie.

Admittedly the iPad isn't the most convenient device for regular photography as it is a very different size and

shape to a regular camera, which means it isn't discreet and may be tricky in getting the exact angle you're after, but it's well-equipped nonetheless and produces good results. It also features video stabilisation for shooting on the move, face detection in still images and 'tap to focus' – where tapping an object on screen makes this the focal point of your image.

So which iPad is right for you?

With all things considered, which iPad is the one that would best suit your needs? In considering this, let's start with the new iPad.

Physically, it makes very little difference which model you choose. Whether or not you opt for 4G, your iPad will measure 241.2 x 185.7 x 9.4mm. The 4G edition, though, is 10g heftier than its wifi-only sibling, tipping the scales at 662g, as opposed to just 652g.

Opt for the iPad 2, on the other hand, and the wifi-only model will be 241.2 x 185.7 x 8.8mm in size (height x width x depth). Adding 3G features will increase the weight by just 12g to 613g, which in day-to-day use will be barely noticeable. It will also add a plastic strip to the top of the rear panel to house the SIM. Otherwise, the two lines are identical.

A more meaningful 'size' measurement is your iPad's capacity. As we have outlined, there are three capacities to choose from, with each step up double the size of its

predecessor. Fortunately, doubling the capacity doesn't simultaneously double the price.

It's tempting to immediately opt for the highest capacity you can afford, but by thinking carefully about the way you'll use your iPad you can save yourself a tidy sum, which you can then put towards some apps.

So, what does each one mean in real-world use? Most iOS applications are fairly small, and you could expect to fit around 50 average size downloads into just 5GB. Assuming a 4MB file size for a regular music file, even the 16GB model would give you enough space to store around 4,000 tracks – about 400 albums-worth – if you didn't use it for anything else. Most users could therefore afford to start by looking at the lower end of the scale and work up from there, and only consider the 32GB and 64GB models if they are sure they will be installing a lot of games or copying videos from their Mac or PC for viewing on the move.

Do bear in mind, of course, that a small portion of the capacity of each iPad will be consumed by the operating system and default applications, such as Contacts, Mail, Calendar and so on. In real world use, therefore, you won't have the full capacity available for your own use.

Refurbished iPads

Scroll down to the bottom of Apple's online store and you'll find a link to its Refurb Store. For those in the know, this is a shopping gem. It offers significant discounts on current products, and you can often make a saving of up to 50% on some slightly older goods.

You shouldn't be shy to buy refurbished products direct from Apple, or from its authorised third-party resellers who often provide a similar service.

Any product bought from the Refurb Store – including iPads – will have been thoroughly checked over by Apple and will be supplied with a warranty, so you can return it for Apple to sort out should it develop any problems.

Refurbished goods are supplied with all of the add-ons that would have originally shipped with the product, including any necessary adaptors, cables and manuals.

Previous-generation iPads

Apple currently supports the original and second-generation iPads, but it won't do so indefinitely.

iOS 5.1, the operating system update that shipped on the same day as the new iPad, was a free update for anyone using an original iPad or iPad 2, and there's no indication from Apple yet that future editions won't continue to be available for those products. If you're not too worried about the speed increases in both processor and graphics hardware that you'll enjoy when you buy new iPad, you might therefore consider buying an iPad 2.

This can deliver real cost savings. On the day it announced the new iPad, Apple immediately dropped the price of the original iPad, while simultaneously slimming down the range from three models to just one 16GB variant with both wifi-only and 3G capabilities. Third-party resellers are likely to do the same as their stocks run down, and this will continue until supplies are exhausted or Apple chooses to stop producing new units, at which point the second hand market will be the only legitimate channel through which to buy them.

Should you buy one? In the short term, the answer is yes. The iPad 2 remains a very capable device. It will be a little slower as it features an older processor than the new iPad, and so lacks the graphics boost of the latest iteration. If you're not playing games, though, that probably won't be a great concern.

However, the most noticeable difference will be the fact that the iPad 2 lacks the Retina Display of the new model, and so you won't experience such sharp graphics.

However, there is a more serious consideration to bear in mind: software compatibility. Some owners of the original iPhone are starting to find that some applications don't work on their handsets. This is either because Apple is no longer shipping iOS updates for their device, meaning that applications that use the operating system's most advanced features are beyond their reach, or because the hardware is no longer up to the job. This will happen with the iPad, too. As Apple ships ever more advanced units, the chance of all applications working on the original iPad and iPad 2 will get ever slimmer.

If you don't plan on regularly upgrading your device with each new release, then it is probably worthwhile spending the small amount extra you need to splash out to bag yourself the latest, greatest device and make savings in the longer term when you don't need to buy the next iteration just to keep up with advances in downloaded applications.

Which iPad is right for you?

If you haven't yet bought an iPad, there are several factors that you should consider before reaching for the credit card. Answering the following three questions will help you rule out those that don't meet your requirements leaving you with the iPad that perfectly suits your needs.

- Will you always (or almost always) have access to a wireless network? If so, you can save money by ruling out the 4G models. Unless...

- Will you be travelling away from home, in which case a 4G model with a contract may be a better option as you'll not have to use public hotspots.

- Are you happy to take only a subsection of your music and videos with you? If so, opt for a cheaper, lower capacity iPad and synchronise more often, archiving media that you won't use back to your Mac or PC.

10 reasons...

...to buy yourself an iPad. If you're having trouble justifying the cost of an iPad in these cash-strapped times, then let us help you shake off that burden of financial guilt as we walk you through the most compelling reasons to invest...

A re you having difficulty justifying your purchase of an iPad? You've lived this long without one, after all, so why should the appearance of a smart new gadget from Apple mean you can't live a moment longer without splashing out?

If you need to justify to yourself – or indeed your partner, parents or children – why you should invest in an iPad for your own enjoyment, here are the top ten reasons for buying one of these sleek, beautiful, digital slates – or, indeed, for upgrading from the original or second-generation model to a new iPad.

Battery life

If you're going to watch films without interruption, you need to be sure that your battery won't run dry half way through. Tests and reviews have consistently shown that Apple's claims of around 10 hours' Internet-based use on a single charge are realistic. This is thanks in part to the low-drain components, but also to the smart, pared-down operating system under the hood that's been tailored to provide the functions you need, without excess, in the most efficient way for the processor and surrounding hardware.

No network fees

With two models to choose from, Apple gives you the choice of a 4G- or wifi-only iPad. While the wifi-only device won't be able to access the Internet, email and other online resources when you're away from your home or office network, the fact that you won't be signed up to

a cellular provider means you won't be tied into an ongoing monthly contract. You can use all of the iPad's most innovative features for free on your own network.

Perfect for dummies

The iPad is a sealed unit. That means you don't need to worry about upgrading it over time or diagnosing problems with the operating system. Every application is vetted by Apple, so it remains virus- and glitch-free, and your computing experience will be smooth and easy. It's perfectly safe and ideal for anyone who wants to actually *use* their computer, rather than maintain it.

Built-in applications

Unpack your iPad, switch it on and you're ready to go. The iPad comes preinstalled with a wide range of first-class applications that will handle your most common tasks – email, browsing, organising your photos and so on – without you having to install or pay for any more software.

Easy software upgrades

But what about all those applications that don't come as standard? Well, you're sorted there, too, with the inclusion of the App Store on the iPad home screen. Apple has built itself a well-managed ecosystem that surrounds the iPhone, iPod and now iPad, with hundreds of third-party developers around the world working on software for these devices, ready to be installed automatically with one tap of your finger.

iPad-unique applications

Although the iPad will run every iPhone application, several hundred thousand have been written purely for the iPad, to take advantage of its bigger screen and other dedicated features. That number includes Apple's own office suite, iWork, which has been ported from the Mac to the iPad. These have latterly been joined by three key applications from iLife, so now you can use iPhoto, iMovie and GarageBand on the move, too.

Dump your desktop Mac (or PC)

Thanks to its optional Dock with keyboard, you can use your iPad as a fully-fledged desktop computer. Because it's designed to sit in the stand in portrait orientation it offers a view of your work that isn't available to the regular computer user, who must spend more of their time scrolling their pages up and down to get an overview of any document. Third-party manufacturers have produced their own alternatives to the dedicated iPad keyboard, giving you a wider choice, and you can even use the wireless keyboard that Apple bundles with many of its desktop computers.. Tap around a few of them until you find the one that's most comfortable for your typing style.

With one of these sitting before it on the desk, and the iPad propped up so that you can easily see the screen, it can quickly become a work-anywhere device, allowing you to tap out notes on the train using the on-screen keyboard, and then switch to the desktop keyboard to finish your work when you get to the office.

Bright, big screen

If you want to watch movies on the move, you can squint at your iPhone or iPod touch, but imagine how much better it would be to enjoy them as Hollywood intended – on a bright, wide screen. The iPad's 9.7in display is perfect for on-the-move entertainment, helping your daily commute fly by, and even better with the new iPad's high-resolution retina display.

A better iPhone experience

The iPad can do almost everything an iPhone can, with one crucial difference: it doesn't make calls. That isn't surprising, considering its size, but it does mean that all of your favourite iPhone features will be bigger and easier to use. If you have trouble typing on your iPhone, the iPad should solve that problem and your productivity should increase by an order of magnitude. Games, too, benefit from the bigger screen, giving you a better view of rendered scenes and more space in which to tap the controls.

The best of the web... made better

Think of the web's most innovative features, and improve on them. That's what Apple has done with the iPad. The dedicated YouTube application wraps up the web's best video sharing site in a fully-fledged interface, making it easier to search and enjoy user videos. Likewise, the Maps application simplifies Google Maps, letting you switch in an instant between plan and satellite views, and follow directions wherever your intended destination.

Even the browser itself is smarter than the average desktop client. It's fully aware of the dimensions of the page it's displaying, allowing you to double-tap on elements on the page to zoom them until they fill the screen. It has multiple tabs, built-in bookmarking, and can synchronise your reading list with a Mac for an all-round first-class performance.

But what about Flash?

It is now a well-known fact that Apple has not authorised Adobe's Flash player for use on the iPad, iPhone or iPod touch. Flash is used by many online websites, applications and games as a means of providing real-time interactivity. It's present on close to 100% of desktop and laptop computers. Apple would argue that it is not required on iOS devices such as the iPad because HTML5 provides many of the same features in a lighter, native way, and in many cases that's true, as can be seen in online applications such as iCloud at *icloud.com* and Google Calendar. In practice, the absence of Flash on the iPad will impact very few users, but that hasn't stopped a lot of rivals, who did support Flash, using it as a selling point for their devices. This may well change in the future as Adobe is scaling down its work on mobile versions of Flash as the company spends more time expanding its impressive stable of HTML5 development applications.

iPad v iPhone

Sure, they look similar, and the iPad can run iPhone apps, but that doesn't mean they have equivalent features. Ideally we'd each have both, but if you can't afford that, then the question is, which is the right choice for you?

The iPad is more than just an oversized iPhone (or, indeed, an oversized iPod touch). Beyond the obvious size mismatch, there are significant differences to the way in which each one works and what they can do. How do you choose?

Communication

The big question is: do you need to make calls on your mobile device? If the answer is yes, then the iPad is not for you as its cell connection is only used for data transfer, not for voice calls. You can, however, run FaceTime over the wifi network and exchange net-based text messages with iOS and OS X users courtesy of the iMessage app.

User Experience

What are you going to use your iPad for if not for working with words and numbers? Pictures? Movies? TV shows downloaded from the iTunes Store?

In all of these respects the iPad wins out. The 9.7in screen is perfect for watching videos without being so large that you're encroaching on the seat of the commuter beside you. And when it comes to photos, the iPad is remarkably close to the size and shape of a picture frame, allowing you to show off your shots to friends and family without everyone having to crowd around or pass the device from person to person.

With the inclusion of two cameras on the iPad 2 and new iPad, even capture is no differentiator. Previously the iPhone had a lead here, thanks to the two cameras found on opposite sides, but not any more.

Size and specs

The most obvious difference between the two devices is their physical size. The iPad is far larger than the iPhone, yet slimmer. The processor has better graphics-handling capabilities, and more cores among which to spread the work.. The iPhone's good, but not that good.

The primary downside of all this additional real-estate is the loss of portability. You can easily carry around the iPad on your day-to-day travels if you're happy to put it into a bag, but not if you want to leave that bag at home and slip your primary communications tool into your pocket. Here, the iPhone is the clear winner. It isn't much larger than a very plain calls-and-texts-only phone yet boasts the features of a full-blown computer. The iPad, on the other hand, even with just the SmartCover, would only fit into an unnaturally large coat pocket.

Which should you buy?

So what is right for you? An iPhone or an iPad? As ever, your choice should be determined not so much by bragging rights, but by what you want to do with your chosen device.

If your primary intention is to consume media, either online or locally on your chosen device, then the iPad is unquestionably the better choice. It's also more accomplished when it comes to doing 'proper' work thanks to the larger screen.

The two places the iPhone wins is in the photography stakes, with both a better camera, and the phone functionality.

Chapter 2
iPad applications

Native applications

Even if you choose not to buy any third-party applications, you will find plenty of high quality software installed on your iPad when you take it out of the box. Here's what you get for your money.

T he iPad, like the iPhone and iPod touch, comes preloaded with a range of essential applications, helping you stay in touch on the move, play your media, chat with (and email) friends, family and business contacts, and control the iPad's settings. Even if you never venture onto the App Store there's plenty to keep you busy.

Communication

The iPad doesn't have any phone functionality, perhaps because Apple doesn't want us all to think of it as little more than an oversized iPhone, but it does have four killer communication tools built in: Mail, Safari, FaceTime and Messages.

Safari

Safari (*right*) is available for the Mac, Windows, iPhone, iPod touch and iPad. It is one of the first five browsers to appear in Windows 7's browser selection screen, which means over time it will become more widely used – good news for iPad users who'll benefit from better support.

The real benefit of browsing on the iPad, though, is that web sites are traditionally laid out in a vertical manner, with pages far longer than they are wide. By using the iPad in portrait orientation you'll be able to view pages from top to bottom with less scrolling, and turning the tablet through 90 degrees to landscape orientation will zoom the page to fit the width. The latest iteration of iOS also introduced Safari's Reader view, which strips out adverts and page clutter so you can focus on the content.

Mail

Mail (*right*) is one of the most attractive email applications on any platform, and being sensitive to the orientation of the iPad it will redraw its interface in one of two ways to make best use of the available space. It won't stumble on attachments. The most common file types are handled with aplomb, saving you from waiting until you get to a fully-featured desktop or laptop before you can open attached PDF documents, Word files, images and so on.

The iPad's Mail application will be instantly familiar to anyone who uses a Mac on a day to day basis as it's almost identical to the application of the same name that ships as a part of Mac OS X.

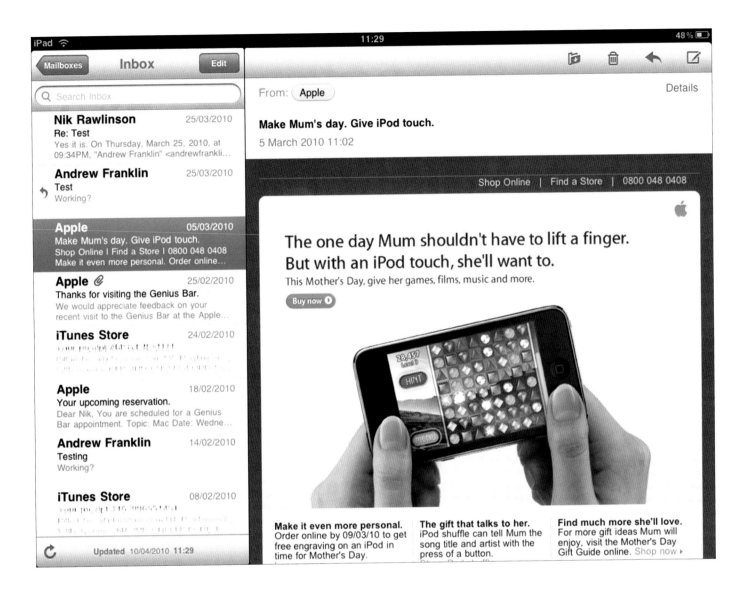

FaceTime

Putting the front and rear cameras to good use, FaceTime is a wifi-based video calling system that lets you make Internet calls to friends and family with an iPhone 4 or later, iPod touch, Mac with FaceTime camera or other iPad (iPad 2 and later only).

You use the front camera to address them directly, and can tap an icon to switch to the rear-mounted device to give them a view of what you can see behind the iPad. Best of all, all calls made on FaceTime are free.

Messages

Messages first appeared on the iPhone 4 but has now been extended to the iPad, iPod touch and Mac and allows users to send free messages to each other over Apple's servers, with all notes in either direction synchronised so that they appear on every platform. As far as the iPad is concerned, this is the closest you'll get to sending SMS text messages.

Media

The iPad has changed the way we consume media for ever. With all the great features of iTunes, 'Music' and 'Videos', and the added bonus of iBooks its an end-to-end media playback device. It can even broadcast that media to your widescreen TV courtesy of Apple TV and AirPlay. Plus, with the option for publishers to create their own bespoke applications for sale through Newsstand, it looks set to become the vital shot in the arm required by newspaper and magazine publishers worldwide.

Music

Once named 'iPod' after Apple's iconic range of portable music players, the Music app brings your iTunes library to your tablet. No longer do you have to scroll through a list of tracks and artists, and neither do you have to flick through your album covers one by one in CoverFlow. Thanks to Music on the iPad you can view your music library as a collection – just like you do at home. Whether you're using it in landscape or portrait mode, your album covers are presented in all their glory, while a category list on the left hand side, including Podcasts, Audiobooks and your own playlists, lets you navigate easily between different media types.

It has Genius built in, so can draw up on-the-fly playlists of tracks that go well together, so you'll always hear a fresh stream of music suited to your particular tastes. Songs are loaded onto your iPad through iTunes, on either your Mac or PC, or on the iPad itself. Tracks you buy directly from the iTunes Store on the iPad will be synchronised back to your computer the next time you connect by USB, or wirelessly over iCloud.

iTunes

iTunes is your window on the iTunes Store, giving you access to an unrivalled collection of music and movies. Unlike the Mac- and PC-based version, it isn't a playback application. It is also the tool that will manage how and where you access your downloads, synchronising what you have bought between the iPad and your main computer every time you dock the two.

YouTube

YouTube is the web's best-known movie sharing site, and the YouTube application (*below*) builds on its success. Rather than presenting you with a view of the site in its native format, it wraps it up in an attractive interface, helping you to find related content whenever you finish watching an uploaded video.

Because of the size of its screen you can also watch higher-definition videos in their best possible quality, so for any YouTube addicts who spend a lot of time watching posted movies on their iPhone or iPod touch, this one feature could well be enough to justify the cost of upgrading to the new iPad on its own.

Videos

If you've ever watched a video on an iPhone or iPod, you'll know what it feels like to wish you had some extra space. In that case, the iPad may be the answer to your prayers. You can buy films and TV shows directly on the

iPad through the iTunes Store or synchronise them to the device from iTunes on your Mac or PC. When you've done so, you can skip straight to specific points and navigate to chapters, just like you can with a DVD.

The iPad's battery really comes into its own here, allowing you to watch up to 10 hours of video on the go, so no matter how delayed your commute might be, you probably won't want the journey to end.

Photos

The iPad gives you simply the best photo viewing experience, bar none. It's easy to get your photos from a Mac or PC onto the device and, once there, show them off to family and friends. iPad 2 and later can take their own photos, and Apple also makes two adaptors: one for connecting your camera directly to the iPad, and one for inserting a media card.

The Photos application arranges your shots in stacks which, when tapped, open up to show the pictures each

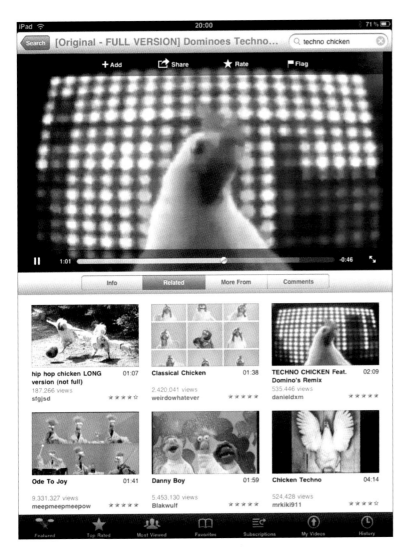

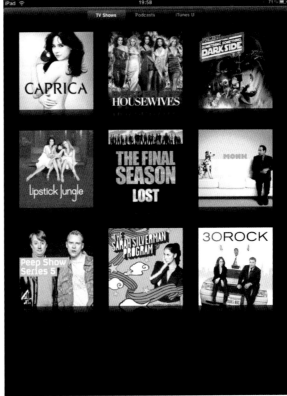

one contains. With a 9.7in screen in your hands you have a bigger viewing window than is presented by most digital photo frames, so it's not surprising that it's great for gathering friends around to look at your photos.

Photo Booth

Photo Booth first appeared on the Mac where it used the built-in iSight camera to present a live view of the person sitting before it, which could then be manipulated in a number of amusing ways, warping and twisting the image.

Thanks not only to its cameras but also its powerful processor and impressive graphics performance, the iPad can now do the same, presenting nine live streams that you can manipulate at will, actually moving the point of distortion in real time by dragging it with your finger. It's a bit of fun, of course, but one that actually works better on the iPad than its original Mac edition.

Productivity

The iPad is more than a cool media player. It's also a fully-fledged business and productivity device, as evidenced by the fact that Apple has rewritten its Pages, Numbers and Keynote office tools to run on its smaller screen. They are charged-for downloads and don't come preinstalled, but four essential business tools will appear on your home screen from day one.

Calendar

Calendar applications are among the oldest uses of personal digital assistants, of which the iPad is so far the ultimate evolutionary point. Its built-in calendar application is arguably the best portable day book since the Filofax, with daily, weekly, monthly and list views and a beautiful interface that mimics regular paper-based diaries and spiral-bound calendars, depending on your orientation and view (*above*).

The application's name is slightly misleading, because it's not one single calendar, but a whole host of them, each colour coded so they can be displayed simultaneously, without you getting confused about which appointment relates to which.

Contacts

The iPad is a great emailing device, which allows you to keep in touch with your friends, family and business

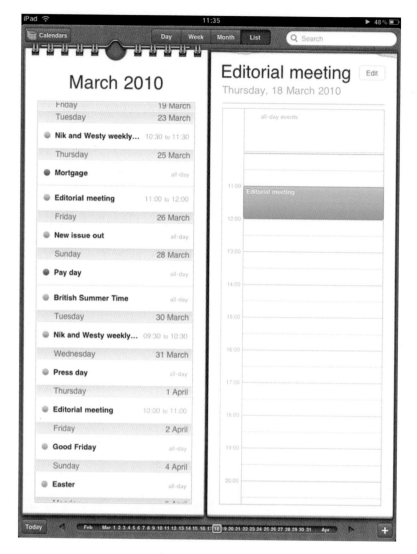

associates wherever you happen to be. The Mail application is therefore backed up by a comprehensive address book called Contacts.

This opens like a traditional address book, with an indexed list of names on the left-hand side, and each of your contacts on the right. This right-hand page is highly reminiscent of the Mac OS X Address Book, and it can organise multiple email addresses and phone numbers for each contact, a generous clutch of notes, and even a photo to help you visualise them when you're composing a message in your head. You can also add birthday reminders that will appear in the Calendar application's birthday calendar if you have it active.

Contacts can be searched either from within the application itself, or using the Spotlight tool, which will drag in information from every application on your iPad,

Maps is more than a digital atlas, though: it's also a constantly-updated guidebook that knows exactly where you are. Thanks to your iPad's built-in GPS receiver, the data from which can be combined with triangulation data from the mobile phone network and the IP details of connected wifi networks, Maps can show you exactly where you are, whether you are using the street view or satellite images. Once you know that, you can start to use its intelligent search tools.

These could be as commonplace as directions that plot the best route between where you are and where you want to go, or as complex as a series of map pins showing the nearest petrol stations, doctors' offices, pizza houses or branches of Starbucks.

With an iPad and the Maps application you really can throw away your atlas, which is out of date almost as soon as it's printed anyway, and with Safari waiting in the wings you can chuck out your guidebook, too. Lightweight 21st century travelling starts here.

Notes

You don't need to wait for a 'killer application' to justify the iPad: Apple has already provided it by porting its successful iWork suite of word processing, spreadsheet and presentation tools to the platform. Sadly they aren't installed by default, and must be bought separately. However, that's not to say that you can't use the iPad as a writing tool, because the basic but capable Notes application goes some way to plugging the gap.

Notes first appeared on the iPhone and then, on launch, the iPod touch. It looks like an American legal jotter with ruled yellow pages bound at the top, and with a margin running down the left-hand edge. When you type onto them your words appear in a marker pen font that looks like very neat handwriting.

You can keep as many notes as you like, and although they aren't well organised (they appear in reverse order of creation, with the most recent at the top) you can search their contents either within the Notes application itself or using the system-wide Spotlight search tool.

Notes is one of the iPad's native applications whose interface changes as you rotate the device. Hold your iPad in portrait orientation and the page takes over the whole screen, with a *Notes* button in the top left hand corner that, when tapped, drops down a list of pages in your

making it easy for you to see not only a contact's address and phone details, but also any email threads shared between you.

Records can be organised into groups, allowing you to keep all of your work, club and personal contacts separate and scroll through each one quickly without the clutter in each of the others.

Maps

You must be online to use the Maps application as it draws its data from Google's map servers. This is no real hardship as it means you can view not only a street plan but also high resolution satellite imagery (*above*), which looks so much better on the iPad's larger screen than it does on a poky iPhone or iPod touch display, giving you a better overview of the surrounding area.

notepad. Turn it through 90 degrees and hold it in landscape orientation, however, and you'll see that your notepad appears in an attractive leather folder with a pocket to the left, inside of which a slip of paper shows a list of your notes.

Four buttons at the foot of the notepaper let you flick back and forth through the pages, bin the note you're working on or send it via email using Mail.

System

Apple thinks it knows how your iPad should be configured, but perhaps you have other ideas. The three core system applications installed natively on every iPad let you make the device easier to use, more functional with downloaded applications, and easier to navigate thanks to a powerful internal search engine.

Accessibility

The Accessibility application, found through the Settings app, lets you switch audio from stereo to mono, speak corrections every time it automatically changes your input, invert the display for improved legibility, zoom in on particular areas, and announce the elements that your fingers pass over.

Further accessibility features found in other applications that ship with the iPad include a screen reader and closed captioning for digital media playback.

App Store

Let's face it: the iPad's native applications are great, but the novelty would soon wear off if they were the start and end of all you could do with your new gadget. That was the case with the iPhone when it was first launched and Apple announced that if anyone wanted to develop apps for it they would have to do so through the browser. There was a minor backlash and, when buyers started to unlock their iPhones so that they could install whatever they wanted, Apple's hand was forced. It released a software development kit so that commercial coders could finally develop for the platform.

A variation on that development kit works on the iPad, allowing those same developers to retool their apps to take advantage of the iPad's bigger screen, and even if they should choose not to do so, native iPhone apps will run on the device. This is good news, as it means that on

launch day the iPad already had access to around 150,000 third-party applications, each of which downloadable from the integrated App Store.

You can manage your downloads through iTunes on your Mac or PC, or directly from your iPad. Both let you search through the full catalogue and pay for downloads without using your credit card, whose details are accessed using a unique Apple ID. Thanks to iCloud, they can also be set to synchronise automatically.

The App Store icon is dynamic. It doesn't just give you access to the application itself, but also tells you about the state of your iPad, notifying you when updates are available for programs you have downloaded in the past by applying a small badge to the upper right corner containing a digit showing the number of updates waiting to be downloaded.

Spotlight

Spotlight is Mac OS X's search tool. It finally appeared on the iPhone and iPod touch with the version 3.0 software update. Now it appears on the iPad, too, and is accessed by swiping the home screens all the way to the left.

Spotlight loves to search, and it doesn't care where it's looking. Start typing in its input box and it immediately heads off around your iPad gathering up matching information – everything from notes and contacts to appointments and messages sitting in your inbox. As you keep typing, it keeps searching so that while it might pull up a lot of contacts and incoming emails as you type 'dan', they could well disappear when you type another three letters to complete the word 'danger'.

This saves you the responsibility of keeping track of where you have filed your data. You simply need to do your work and be creative, and leave the filing up to your iPad and Spotlight, which appears both as its own application and as a tool in applications like Mail.

And... iBooks

Eagle-eyed readers will spot that this e-reading application has almost the same name as Apple gave to its range of low-end portable computers.

iBooks downloads reading matter from the online iBookstore and also lets you add your own books in ePub format from your computer. It's a beautiful electronic book reading application with crisply-rendered text and full colour images.

Apple is helping authors to create stunning content for the app, courtesy of its own free OS X application called iBooks Author.

This is clearly Apple's riposte to the Kindle, which Amazon is hoping will turn us all on to digital- rather than paper-based reading, and in some (but not all) respects the experience is superior. The most obvious difference is the colour screen. Some users may be put off by the shiny surface when comparing it directly to the Kindle's matt surface, which is the price you pay for colour.

iBooks is not installed on the iPad by default. In the countries in which Apple has signed agreements to distribute books through the iBookstore, the application is a free download from the App Store, and you're prompted to install it the first time you enter the Store.

There's more

Over the coming pages, we'll take a closer look at the most compelling native iPad applications, before going on to show you how you can download and install your own, and show you how you ways to use them.

By the time we get to the end, you will see just how flexible this remarkable device is, thanks to the tireless and ever-expanding community of developers working to write software for you.

Mail

The iPad offers one enormous step up from the iPhone when it comes to handling your email. Here we take a look at its most prominent features and how you can put it to best use.

E mail is one of the most important tools for any mobile worker. RIM discovered that when it released the Blackberry, which offered its owners always-on email access wherever they were. The Blackberry was a smash hit, for both business and home users. Apple followed suit with the email application in the iPhone and iPod touch, and now it's done the same with the iPad, with a first-class email client that really makes the best use of the available screen space.

Hold it horizontally and you will see a split screen, with either your folders or the contents of your selected mailbox in the left-hand column (*right*). The main part of the screen, to the right of this, is where the content of your email will be, whether you're reading or writing.

Open a mailbox by tapping on it, and the top of the message list will sport a useful search box, allowing you to hunt through your messages for particular content, without having to open up each one individually.

If you turn the iPad to portrait orientation, the screen looks quite different. The whole display spins around, with the static mailboxes or message list swivelling off the left hand side, and a new toolbar appearing at the top of the screen. This has the same controls for filing, deleting and forwarding a message at the right hand side, alongside the new message button on the far right, but to the left it there is now also an inbox button and up and down controls. These controls step forwards and backwards through messages (*see far right*).

The inbox button is of most use, as tapping it drops down a list of your incoming messages, allowing you to skip straight to the one you need without stepping through those that appear around it. It also reinstates the search box.

However you display the inbox contents, whether as a permanent panel running down the screen beside your message body or in this floating overlay, you will see an Edit button at the top. This button is key to controlling the contents of your mailbox and maintaining a proper filing system.

In the grab below, we're sitting at the top level of the Mail interface, with our mailboxes on display. Tapping the accounts in the top half of the column takes us straight to the inbox for each one; tapping those that appear in the Accounts section displays the folders inside each one.

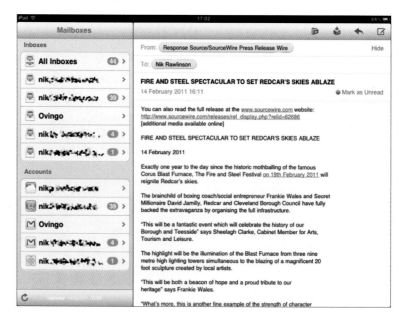

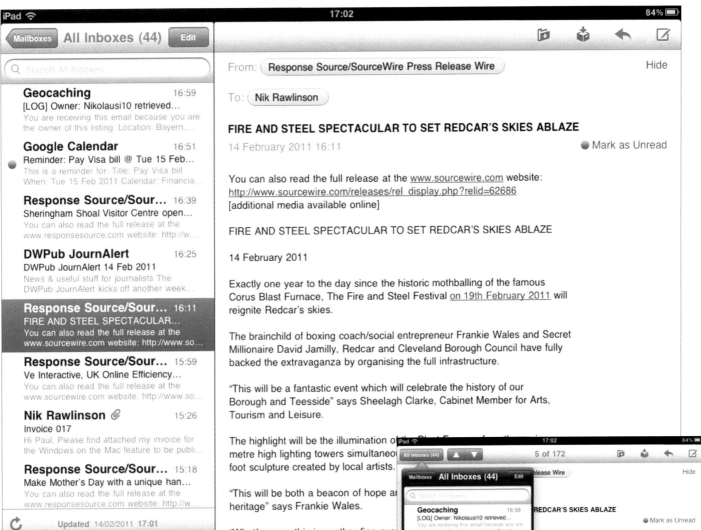

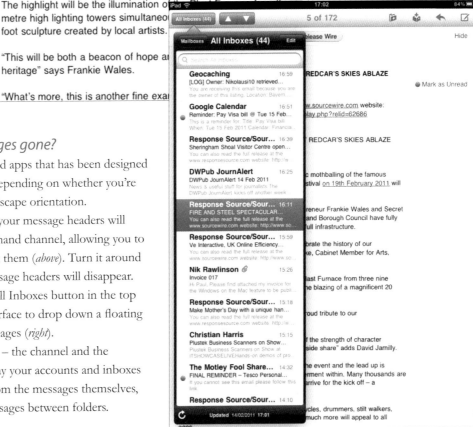

Where have my messages gone?

Mail is one of the native iPad apps that has been designed to work in a different way depending on whether you're holding it in portrait or landscape orientation.

Hold it horizontally and your message headers will always be visible in the left-hand channel, allowing you to immediately switch between them (*above*). Turn it around by 90 degrees and your message headers will disappear. To get them back, tap the All Inboxes button in the top left-hand corner of the interface to drop down a floating dialogue showing your messages (*right*).

These interface elements – the channel and the drop-down – will also display your accounts and inboxes when you step up a level from the messages themselves, or when you're moving messages between folders.

How to delete multiple messages

There are two ways to delete single messages from your inbox. You can either tap the trash icon on the menu bar or, if that's not present, swipe a single finger across the message header in the inbox listing in the left-hand column to call up the *Delete* or *Archive* button (*see below*).

This isn't a practical solution if you need to delete a lot of emails at once, though, as it would take you far too long to step through each one. Fortunately, though, there is a simple way to delete several messages at once and save yourself a lot of swiping and tapping.

Look at the top of your message list for the *Edit* button (step back into your inbox if you can only see the list of your mailboxes in the left-hand column).

Tap the button and all of your messages will shift to the right to make space for a column of lozenges. As you tap each one – and you can tap more than one in sequence – you will select the message beside it. You can then delete the selected messages by tapping the red delete button at the foot of the column.

Notice how every message that you've selected to delete is stacked up in the right-hand window so that you can preview it before wiping it from your iPad. If you change your mind about removing one from your mailbox, tap its lozenge in the left-hand panel for a second time to clear it, and it will be removed from the deletion stack. This works even if the message is not displayed on the top of the stacked queue.

If you don't want to delete the messages, but instead move them to another mailbox, tap the Move button at the bottom of the column and you will be returned to the overall mailbox view. Here, tap on the mailbox into which you want to move the selected messages. See the tip opposite for a quicker way to move just one message at a time between mailboxes on your iPad.

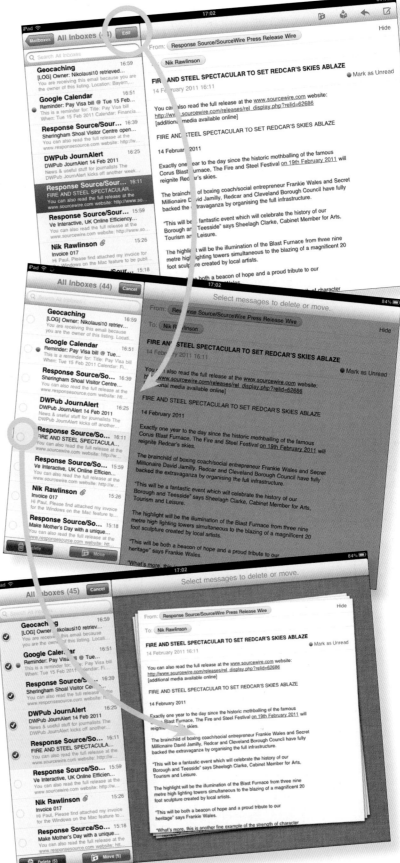

The iPad keyboard

It may look too slimmed-down, but the iPad keyboard is highly versatile. Tap the *123* button to either side of the keyboard, and then #+= to pull up its extended character set. The keyboard icon hides the keys themselves to give over the whole of your screen to the body of your email.

How to set up a signature

Save yourself some time by setting an automatic signature to appear on the bottom of each of your emails. This isn't done through the Mail application itself, but through the central iOS Settings app.

Tap *Mail, Contacts, Calendars* and scroll down to Signature (*left*). Tap this and set your signature in the box that appears, finally tapping the left-pointing arrow above it when you have finished.

TIP Add two hyphens and a space on a blank line above whatever signature you choose, as we have done in the image to the left. Why? Because when people reply to your message their email application will strip out your signature to save passing superfluous data backwards and forwards with each new entry in the conversation thread of messages.

How to move messages

When you've read an email, you'll often want to file it in a more appropriate folder than

your inbox. Rather than waiting until you're back at your Mac or PC, do it from your iPad. Tap the first icon in the buttons at the right of the toolbar (the folder with the down-pointing arrow on it) and the message will shrink to the middle of the screen. Your folders appear in a channel on the left. Select the one to which you want to send it. If you need to move it to another account, tap the Accounts button at the top of the list (*below*), select the account you need and, again, choose the relevant folder.

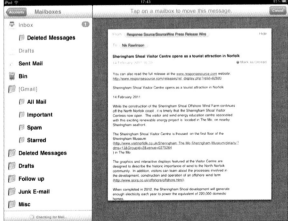

Safari

Apple's web browser now appears on no less than three platforms: the Mac, Windows and iOS devices. Here's how it works on your iPad, and how to save shortcuts to the home screen.

Safari is the iPad's web browser. By default it's found on the springboard so that it appears on every screen, although you can move it elsewhere if you want to use this space for something else.

If you use Safari on the Mac or PC, many of its controls and interface elements will already look familiar. The toolbar that runs across the top of the screen has your forward and back controls, a button for opening new browser windows, the bookmark manager (it looks like an open book) and the shortcut saver (the box with an arrow coming out of it) and then two input boxes: the address box, where you type the address of the page you want to visit, and the search box, where you enter searches you want to send to Google.

While the iPhone / iPod touch edition of Safari retains the discrete screens that this iPad edition also once used (to handle several open pages at a time), since the introduction of iOS 5 the iPad edition now uses tabs in the same way as the regular desktop edition. This lets you tap quickly between them, open new ones by tapping the '+' on the right of the tab bar, and re-order them by dragging each one left and right, at which point all of the others will shuffle to accommodate wherever you drop it.

This mobile edition of Safari is more intelligent than a general desktop or laptop browser, as it knows a lot more about the dimensions of the page you're browsing. Turn it to portrait or landscape orientation and you'll see that it resizes the content to fit the width of the screen, allowing you to choose between a wider or taller display that shows you more of every page. It also knows the dimensions of

everything on the page so that double-tapping any element, such as a column of text or an embedded image, zooms the content until that element takes up the whole width of the screen, whichever way up you have it.

All of Safari's controls are clustered on the toolbar, with many of the buttons sporting drop-down dialogues that reveal hidden features. Tap on the address box and start typing in the URL of the page you want, and a list of matching addresses you have recently visited will drop down so you can pick the one you want without typing the whole address. Likewise, start typing in the search box and it will drop down a list of suggestions and, below the list, any searches you have recently performed that match what you have typed so far. Safari's default search engine is Google, but if you prefer Yahoo or Bing you can switch to either of these through *Preferences | Safari | Search Engine*. Unfortunately you can't specify a localised edition of any engine, so will only see results from the .com version. You should also check the other options in Safari's preferences pages, where you can delete your cookies and clear your browsing history, as well as blocking pop-ups and JavaScript, should you choose.

The bookmarks button (the open book icon) drops down a list of your set bookmarks, at the top of which you'll see an entry for History. This lists all of your recently-visited pages, organised by date so that if you recall visiting a particular page last Monday you can skip straight to it. Your most recently-visited pages are at the top of the list, and older history items are filed into chronological folders to avoid making the list too long.

Shortcuts
Save a page to your bookmarks, or create a shortcut for your iPad home screen and save yourself some typing.

Reload
Click the circular arrow to refresh the page, or to reload it entirely if your iPad had problems downloading it the first time around.

Bookmark / History
Want to keep track of your current page for your next session? Save it as a bookmark or find it in your history through this button.

Tabs
Click to open a new tab. With several tabs open, each displaying a different page, you can switch between them.

How to manage your shortcuts

However good the iPad's on-screen keyboard may be, you don't want to have to type in the address of every page each time you start Safari. For that reason you might want to save your favourites as bookmarks (*see facing page*) and shortcuts.

Shortcuts are a great feature that take you straight to a page from an icon on the iPad home screen, without you needing to manually invoke Safari in the first place. Some sites, such as the Kindle Cloud Reader at *read.kindle.com* and the Financial Times at *ft.com* encourage you to do this for the best user experience.

To place a shortcut on your home screen, fire up Safari and visit the page you need (don't worry – this is the last time you'll have to start the browser yourself).

Tap the shortcut button to the left of the address box. It's a rectangle with an arrow flying out of it. From here you can save a bookmark, email a link to the page, print it to a compatible printer or, of most interest to us, add the page to the home screen. This last one is the option you're after. Tap it to create your shortcut.

Safari will suggest a name for the shortcut, based on the text that appears in the browser title bar. This will most likely be a description of the content rather than the name of the site itself, which the publishers of the site have used to optimise its performance in search engines like Google. Delete the contents of the name box and enter your own. Here, we have chosen *The Guardian*, as that's the site we're saving to the home screen.

When you tap the Add button, your shortcut will be created and dropped into the first available space on your home screen. It will take whichever icon has been set by the site owners.

Tapping this icon will now take you straight to the site, making this an excellent way to access app-like sites such as Gmail and Google Reader. However, you might either tire of the site or find something better in the future, at which point you'll want to remove the shortcut.

Hold down you finger on any icon on your iPad's home screen and wait until all of the icons start to vibrate. Each one will be overlaid by a small 'x' in a circle. Tap this and you will be asked to confirm that you want to delete the shortcut. If you do, tap *Delete* and it will be removed. Tapping *Cancel* leaves it in place. When you have deleted all the links you need, press the iPad home button to exit.

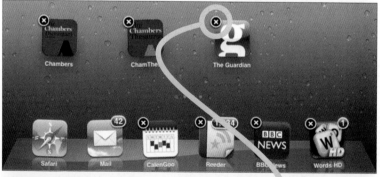

How to save a bookmark

Even if you don't want to create a shortcut for each of your favourite pages, you can still bookmark them to make them easy to find later on. Once again, start by visiting the page you want to save and then tap the shortcut button. This time tap the *Add Bookmark* button.

Again, Safari will suggest a name for the bookmark but you can change this before going on to choose where it is saved. By default it will be saved in your bookmarks folder, but if you will be accessing the page particularly regularly then you might instead want to save it to the Bookmarks Bar, which appears below the address box and gives you one-tap access to your favourite sites. To do this, tap *Bookmarks* at the bottom of the floating dialogue box and then *Bookmarks Bar* in the new dialogue. Tap *Add Bookmark* to complete the process.

The desktop version of Safari lets you drag links straight off the Bookmarks Bar, at which point they disappear in a cloud of smoke. You can't do that on the iPad, but you can still delete them. Tap the Bookmarks button (the open book to the left of the shortcut button) and then tap the Bookmarks Bar within it. This will display all of your existing links. Swipe to the right across the one you want to delete and then tap the red *Delete* button that appears.

How to use Safari's live search

Whichever search engine you have chosen to use with mobile Safari, it can interact with the browser so that you can find the search results you need more quickly through live, updating results.

Start typing in the search box to the right of the address bar, and you'll see that your current page dims and suggestions for what you might be searching for appear in a drop-down dialogue, which extends from the bottom of the search box.

The longer you type, the more accurate the suggestions become as Safari automatically retrieves a refined list from Google, Bing or Yahoo. If it comes up with the answer you're looking for, tap it. If not, tap Search as usual to visit the search engine results listing.

Maps

Who needs an atlas when you've got an iPad? The built in maps tool not only displays global street plans – it also helps you get around by car, bus and foot.

Maps is one of the many iPad tools that relies on third-party services to answer your queries. In this instance, that service is Google's online Maps site, which you can access through a browser at *maps.google.com*.

The Google Maps web site presents highly accurate plan maps and satellite views of the world. You can switch between them and zoom in or out to get a closer look or a more distant overview of an area. You can do the same on the iPad. Tap the curled-up corner in the lower-right of the interface and you'll expose the view menu, which lets you switch between views and turn on or off the traffic overlay. This overlay marks up roads on the map in green, amber and red depending on the state of the traffic so that you can make a decision whether or not to follow a particular route depending on road conditions.

The more you zoom in on the map, the more detail you will see, and as with other applications on the iPad, you zoom in and out by pinching and unpinching the screen. You scroll by dragging your finger across the surface, and to quickly locate yourself on the map, tap the compass arrow icon on the toolbar. This sits beside the address book icon, which lets you tap a contact's name to have the location of their associated address pinpointed on the map.

Maps is more than just a digital atlas, though. It is also a local gazetteer. Find your local area and then search for a business – say a pizza restaurant. Type 'pizza' in the search box and map pins will drop down to locate local

pizza houses in your area. Tap each one to call up their names and when you find the one you want tap the '*i*' icon at the end of each name (*above*). This calls up contact details, including phone numbers and addresses, and options to plot a route either to or from that restaurant.

You can tailor your directions depending on your mode of transport, with options for car, public transport and walking. Each one will be drawn along the shortest appropriate route for that means of travelling, along with estimates of the journey duration. Once you've chosen one, tap *Start* and Maps takes you step by step, turn by turn, through each leg of your journey.

If you decide to take public transport, then be sure to tap the clock icon on the blue information bar. This calls up public transport timetables, taking care of all of your planning for you. By default it will display the next two or three departures. If you don't want to travel right away, choosing a later time is simply a matter of tapping the *Depart* box at the top of the panel and choosing a different time and date, at which point the directions will update to reflect your new departure time.

Unfortunately, in the UK at least, public transport directions are confined to use on foot and bus as our test journeys involving well-known railway commuter routes took convoluted paths along major road networks. Nonetheless, for local travel it is hard to beat.

How to choose different map types

Maps can display four different kinds of map, depending on your needs. Each is provided by Google, and you can switch between them by tapping on the curled up corner in the lower-right of the application. This reveals a menu containing links to the classic map, a photographic satellite view and a terrain view that marks out hills and valleys in 2D using shadows and highlights. Each of these is streamed from the server, with the vector versions likely to load more quickly on a slow link.

There is also a hybrid option, which combines the classic and satellite views to overlay a traditional drawn map on top of photographic satellite imagery to clearly mark out the names of roads.

The option to switch on traffic is only relevant in certain parts of the world. There is fair coverage around major UK cities, where roads will be colour-coded green, amber or red, depending on the weight and speed of traffic using them.

How to find your home on Maps

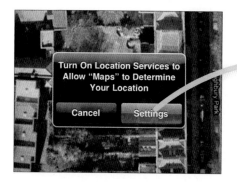
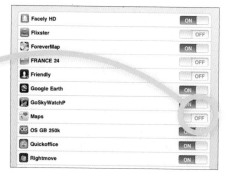

Tap the arrow icon on the Maps toolbar at the top of the screen. If you haven't enabled Location Services for this application you'll see this pop-up warning. Tap *Settings* to switch it on.

You'll be sent to Settings where the Location Services page will be opened. Look for Maps in the list and tap the slider to move it from *OFF* across to *ON*.

Return to the Maps app and a blue pointer will drop on your location. It may initially wander as it gets an accurate fix on your home. The blue circle shows its margin of error.

How to plan a journey with Maps

Maps isn't just about street plans. Double-tap a location on the map and then tap the blue '*i*' on the pin that appears and you can use that as a reference point for mapping a route. Choose whether you want directions to or from that location and then type your origin or destination, as appropriate, in the empty box on the application toolbar.

Maps pulls up the quickest route by road between your two points and tells you both the distance and the time it will take. If you'd rather go by foot or by public transport, tap the pedestrian and bus icons on the blue bar.

The public transport option links in to timetables, so tapping the clock face icon on the bar pulls up a list of the next available departures that would get you to your chosen destination.

If you aren't planning on travelling immediately, tap *Depart* at the top of the floating dialogue and you can specify whether you want to set a time to leave or the time by which you must arrive.

With this done, use the barrels to select a date, hour and minute, and then tap *Done* to confirm.

With your journey now fully defined, by whichever mode of transport, tap *Start* on the blue bar to set off, and use the forwards and backwards arrows that appear to navigate each step of the way.

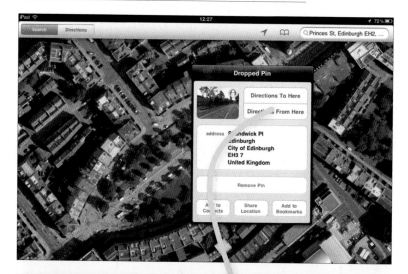
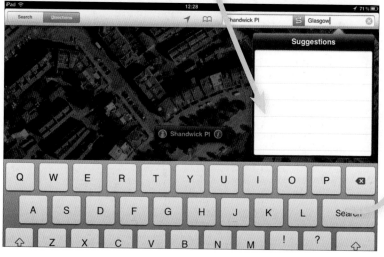

How to use Street View

Google Street view lets you look at a road at ground level. Switch from the regular overhead view by tapping the orange circle on any dropped pin or address, and then navigate the roads by tapping the arrow in the direction you want to travel. Drag your finger on the screen to turn yourself around.

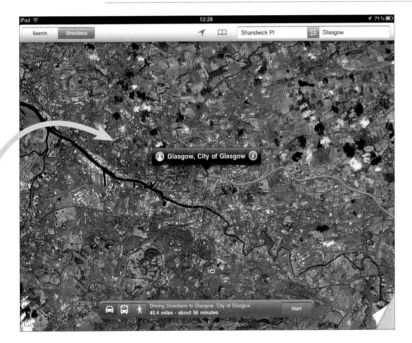

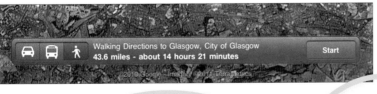

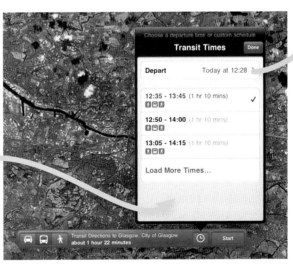

Newsstand

One very special iOS 5 application looks set to breathe new life into papers and magazines. Newsstand makes it easier to find publications you want to read, and keeps your issues up to date.

Apple has already revolutionised the way we buy and consume music, is well on the way to doing the same with movies and TV, and is looking to emulate Amazon's success in the world of digital books, so it's only natural that it should be showing more than a passing interest in magazines.

The iPad is the ideal device on which to consume the next generation of newspapers and mags, as its bright colour screen and extremely thin form factor are both convenient and attractive. No wonder publishers were quick to realise that this could be just the solution they needed to declining print-based audiences. They quickly tooled up a new generation of layout artists and designers with all the kit they needed to create iPad-friendly versions of their existing publications and started selling them through the App Store. They were an immediate success, both converting existing print readers to the digital alternative and finding new audiences right around the world, attracted by the lower prices that resulted from not having to ship printed magazines by air.

The trouble was, if you subscribed to a handful of magazines, and on top of these downloaded as many free titles as you wanted, your iPad home screen could quickly become a cluttered, jumbled mess of icons, each of which looked just like any other app.

Apple came up with a solution: Newsstand. This appears on all iPads, iPhones and iPod touches running iOS 5 or later, and looks like a small set of shelves on your home screen. Tap it to expand the shelves to their full size and you'll see that they are a dedicated home for these magaizne applications, keeping them separate from your real apps and also allowing you to monitor when new issues are ready to download, as each title's cover will be overlaid with a blue strap when it's been updated.

Just like regular apps, magazines can only be downloaded through Apple's dedicated store, accessed from within the Newsstand app. This is good news for avid readers as it means you don't have to think about manually updating your collection or hunting around several shops for the best prices. Better, as all purchases are made using your existing Apple ID all of your payment details are already in place. Keeping up with the news has never been so easy.

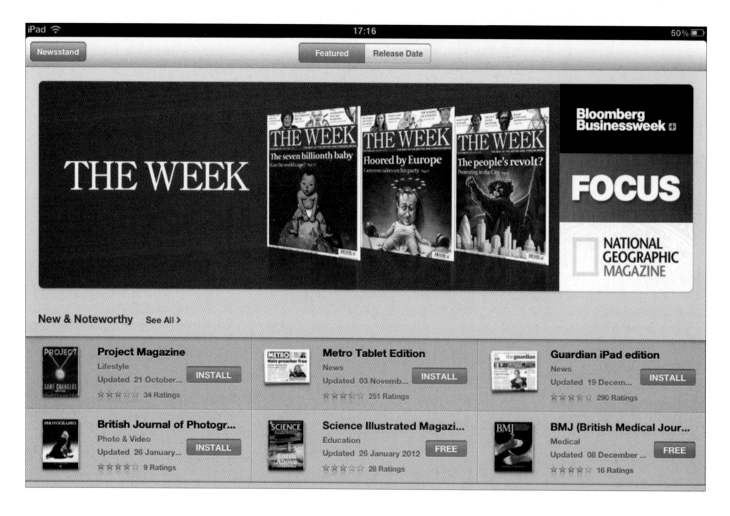

How to buy a magazine on Newsstand

Much like iBooks, Newsstand is tied to its own dedicated store, with the same Apple ID that you use to download applications used to authorise and pay for magazine and newspaper downloads. Get started by tapping the *Store* button on the top of the Newsstand shelves.

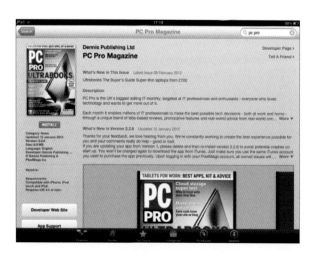

All Newsstand publications will work in a slightly different way, depending on the software that the publisher used to put it together. Here we're going to buy a copy of UK technology title, *PC Pro*. This is served using a system developed by PixelMags, so everything that holds true for this title should also work with others fulfilled using the same back end.

Newsstand publications are technically applications; Newsstand itself is just a clever convention Apple introduced when it rolled out iOS 5 to smarten up the process of buying, reading and managing them, and saving us from having countless publications littering our home screens.

Each one has a dedicated page, just like an app (*left*) detailing any special features, such as interactive content, and giving you a preview of the current edition. Each app is a container for all of the issues of that title that you buy, so you'll only ever see one cover on your Newsstand shelves, no matter how many back issues you own.

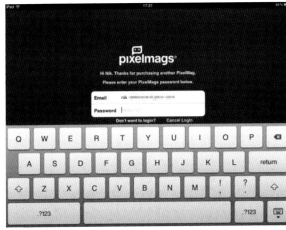

Once downloaded, your free magazine app will appear on your Newsstand shelves (*top left*). Here, you can see that it has a NEW strap on one corner, which indicates that there's a new issue ready for us to download. This happens to all of your Newsstand apps as they are updated, so you needn't keep checking the store.

Most publishers allow you to re-download old editions of magazines you have already bought, so will ask you to set up an account through which they can log your purchases. If this is the first time you have bought a magazine from that publisher, you can create your account when you open the downloaded magazine app for the first time. If you already have an account, you'll be asked to log in, instead (*top right*).

You're now ready to start downloading magazines. The app will present you with a list of available issues, accompanied by their prices and dates of publication. There will also often be options for subscribing for one, three, six or 12 months, which in this instance are detailed

by tapping the *Subscribe* button. For the moment, though, we just want to download a single issue. We have chosen the December 2011 edition of PC Pro. Tapping the price asks us to confirm that we want to buy it, just as the App Store does when we download an application. In this particular magazine app we can track the progress of the download on a drop-down Downloads dialogue (*above left*) through which we can also cancel the download, or repeat it if there was a problem. When the download completes we just need to tap the cover to open it.

Our downloaded magazine looks just the same as the printed version (*above right*), but because it is digital it has a few extra features. Tapping on the screen calls up a strip of thumbnails across the bottom of the pages, allowing us to preview the laid-out spreads and skip straight to the one we want. We can also drop down a list of contents from the toolbar at the top of the screen. The double-ended arrow, meanwhile, lets us loan our copy of this magazine to another user for up to four days.

Music

The device that revived Apple's fortunes may have been the original iMac, but it was the iPod that sparked the company's meteoric ascent. Now it appears in software form on the iPad, in the recently-renamed Music application.

Don't confuse the Music and iTunes applications. On your desktop or laptop computer, you'd use iTunes to listen to your music, but on the iPad (and iPod touch and iPhone) it's only used for downloading content. The Music application is where you'll turn to listen to your music collection, whether bought directly or synchronised from your computer.

Despite this, Music bears more than a passing resemblance to iTunes on a regular computer. The interface is split into two, with library categories running down the left-hand side in a panel of their own, and albums displayed to the right. If you have relevant artwork for your music, they will be displayed like albums on a shelf, or books in the iBooks application. Dragging your finger up and down on the screen scrolls through the albums in your collection.

Below the albums are buttons that let you change the main display to sort your content by song name, artist name, album, genre or composer. The data attached to your tracks that makes this possible is transferred at the same time as your music (if you're filling your iPad from a Mac or PC), or downloaded at the same time as your purchases if you're buying content from the iTunes Store. If you're ripping an existing CD-based music collection to your computer's iTunes library it therefore makes sense to spend time making sure the track names are accurate.

The easiest way to find a track is to use the search box. As you type, it will trim the list of results in the window below. It also greys out some of the buttons at the bottom of the screen to leave only those categories in

which your results appear. The longer you type, the more of these will disappear, but if you still have more than one in full black text, you can tap between them to filter out those items that don't meet your requirements.

Although the library looks quite sparse when you first start using Music on the iPad, you can build it up by creating playlists in which to organise your tracks. Tap the '+' at the bottom of the display and enter a name for your playlist, then to populate it tap the elements you want to include. Again, use the category buttons at the bottom of the screen to switch between artists, albums and so on, selecting tracks from each one. When picking tracks from an album, tap the album's cover art and it will flip over to show you a track listing from which you can select the tracks you want to include.

If you don't have the time or the inclination to build your own playlist, then why not ask your iPad to do it for you. Beside the playlist '+' button you'll see what looks like some neutrons spinning around each other. This is the Genius button. Genius builds playlists of tracks that go well together based on information submitted anonymously by the millions of iTunes users around the world. Tap it and select a starting track, and Music will build a playlist of 25 songs that it thinks will go well together. If you don't like them, tap *Refresh* or, if you think they're perfect, opt for *Save*.

The iPad's built-in speaker is fine for system sounds like alerts and alarms, but might fall short when listening to music unless you're using headphones, or speakers connected to your network using AirPlay.

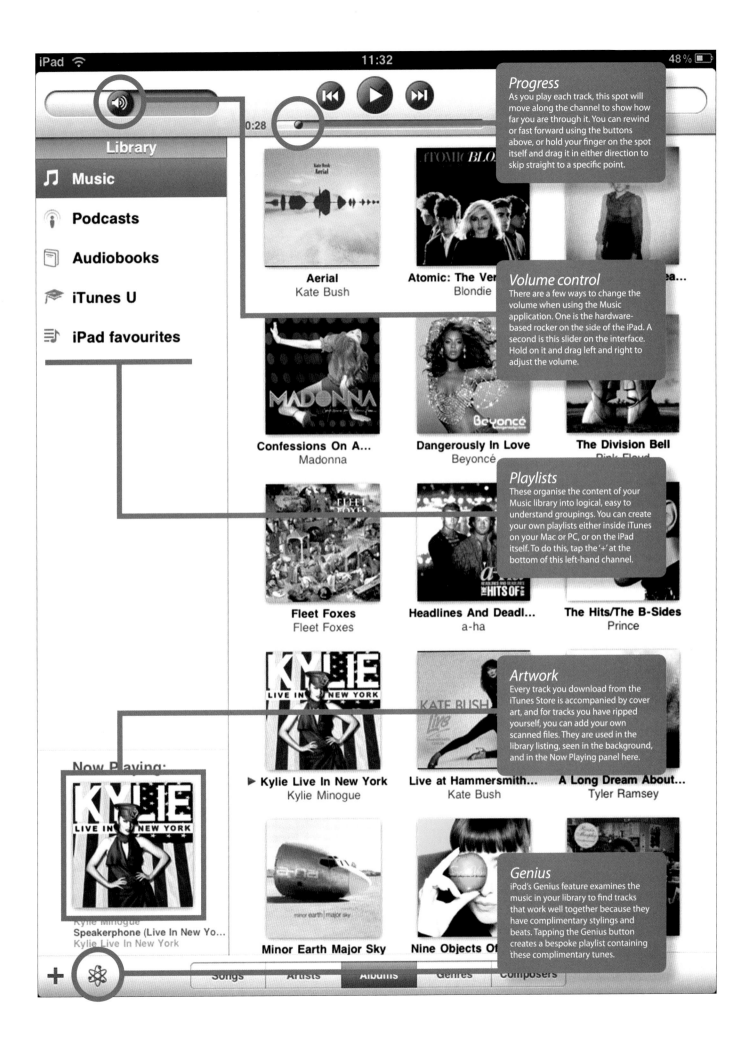

iPad 📶   11:32   48% 🔋

0:28

Library

🎵 Music

🎙 Podcasts

📖 Audiobooks

🎓 iTunes U

🎶 iPad favourites

Aerial
Kate Bush

Atomic: The Ver...
Blondie

Confessions On A...
Madonna

Dangerously In Love
Beyoncé

The Division Bell
Pink Floyd

Fleet Foxes
Fleet Foxes

Headlines And Deadl...
a-ha

The Hits/The B-Sides
Prince

Kylie Live In New York
Kylie Minogue

Live at Hammersmith...
Kate Bush

A Long Dream About...
Tyler Ramsey

Minor Earth Major Sky

Nine Objects Of...

Now Playing:

Kylie Minogue
Speakerphone (Live In New Yo...
Kylie Live In New York

Songs   Artists   Albums   Genres   Composers

Progress
As you play each track, this spot will move along the channel to show how far you are through it. You can rewind or fast forward using the buttons above, or hold your finger on the spot itself and drag it in either direction to skip straight to a specific point.

Volume control
There are a few ways to change the volume when using the Music application. One is the hardware-based rocker on the side of the iPad. A second is this slider on the interface. Hold on it and drag left and right to adjust the volume.

Playlists
These organise the content of your Music library into logical, easy to understand groupings. You can create your own playlists either inside iTunes on your Mac or PC, or on the iPad itself. To do this, tap the '+' at the bottom of this left-hand channel.

Artwork
Every track you download from the iTunes Store is accompanied by cover art, and for tracks you have ripped yourself, you can add your own scanned files. They are used in the library listing, seen in the background, and in the Now Playing panel here.

Genius
iPod's Genius feature examines the music in your library to find tracks that work well together because they have complimentary stylings and beats. Tapping the Genius button creates a bespoke playlist containing these complimentary tunes.

How to build a playlist

Playlists let you gather a collection of your favourite music, or tracks of a certain type such as Christmas music, and organise them into one sorted list, so that you can always get to them without having to search for them or skip backwards and forward through individual entries in your library.

Start by tapping the '+' button at the bottom left of the Music window to create a new playlist, and give it a name.

As soon as you tap Save, your iPad hides the sidebar so you can concentrate on adding tracks to your freshly created playlist.

Use the buttons at the bottom of the screen to switch between songs, artists, albums, genres and composers as you build up a list of your favourite tracks (and they needn't only be songs – you can include spoken word items and audio books, too).

You can use the search box at the top of the screen to narrow down the list of tracks from which you can choose, and the list below it will be thinned as appropriate. Once you've found the tracks you're after, tap each one and it will be added to the playlist, at the same time being greyed out in the listing to that you know it has already been selected and needn't be added twice.

When working with albums you're shown a library of covers, with each one fronted by cover art from the iTunes Store or imported from your PC- or Mac-based iTunes Library.

Tap an album you know to contain tracks you want to use and the artwork will flip over and enlarge to display a scrollable list of the tracks in that album. Again, tap the ones you want to add to your playlist.

To remove tracks from a playlist, open the playlist from the sidebar and tap the Edit button at the top of the screen, then use the red '-' buttons beside each one.

How to explore your albums

You might not think the album view is particularly informative, showing only a grid of your imported or downloaded albums, but it is actually a great piece of design, allowing you to quickly glance across your library to get a feel for what's available, and then tap your chosen album to flip it around and see the tracks it contains. Each one is listed in order, with a track number, name and length, while the currently playing track – if it appears on the selected album – is marked out with a small play triangle in place of its track number.

To step out of the track listing and return to the album overview screen, tap the grey title bar, or anywhere on the screen away from the tracks.

How to enjoy your cover art

It seems such a shame when you have a glorious 9.7in screen at your disposal to only ever view your album art in the grid view, or as a thumbnail in the bottom left corner of the screen when you're playing a track. Tap that thumbnail and the album art expands to fill the whole screen. Tapping it again overlays it with various playback controls. At the top of the screen are the volume, play, forwards and backwards buttons. Below these, the progress bar and, to the left and right respectively, the repeat and shuffle selectors. At the bottom of the screen you'll see three buttons: return to the playlist on the left, build a Genius playlist in the centre, and a button to flip over the artwork and display the album tracks.

How to build a Genius playlist

If you don't want to follow our instructions for building a defined playlist (*see opposite page*) you can assign the task to the Music app. Tap the Genius button at the bottom of the interface and then select a track from your library. Your iPad will examine all of the other tracks in your collection and pick out a list of other tracks that it considers work well alongside it. To do this it uses information submitted anonymously by the millions of iPod, Music and iTunes users around the world, which is analysed centrally and accessed by the iTunes and Music applications. As well as the current track you can see which tracks the Music app has queued, allowing you to skip straight to a favourite entry.

The iPad App Store

The App Store is your gateway to a whole new world of exciting add-ons for your wonderful iPad, but how do you use it? Here, we guide you through the process of buying your first downloaded application.

Installing applications directly to your iPad lets you add to its capabilities when you're away from your home or office, and unable to attach it to your regular Mac or PC.

It's no more difficult than installing through iTunes and uses the same login details, as it's tied to your iTunes Store account. This means that you don't need to store any valuable credit card details in a portable device that you may misplace when out and about.

Better still, if you've set up app synchronisation through iCloud, any apps that you buy on an iPad, iPhone, iPod touch or through iTunes are synchronised to each of your other devices.

The main difference between the way the process works on your regular computer and your iPad is that on the iPad you use the dedicated App Store application rather than purchasing through iTunes, which is only used for buying music and videos.

The App Store has two tabs, allowing you to see what's new and what's popular. If you know what you're after you can safely skip both of these and start typing into the search box on the toolbar (*right*). As you type, it will suggest results. So typing weather, for example, will call up a list of applications that have that word in their title.

When you've found the application you want to install, tap its entry in the list and you'll be presented with a dedicated app page showing you example screen grabs and a short description of its features and capabilities. You can also see how other users have rated it and, crucially, what operating system it requires to work with

your device. Over time Apple will likely issue updates that won't be compatible with all iPads, so this information will become more relevant.

If you want to purchase the application, tap the price or *Free* beneath its icon at the top of the page and you'll see that it changes to read 'Install App'. This is the only confirmation button: you should only tap it if you're happy to commit to buying and installing it on your iPad.

Once you've tapped it you'll leave the App Store (it will keep your place in the background so that next time you re-enter you'll find yourself back at the same page) and install the app, with a progress bar overlaid on its icon showing download progress.

How to install applications, step by step

1. Tap the app's icon in the App Store overview to open its dedicated page. This includes a slideshow of images and a brief description.

2. The *More...* link at the end of the description opens a more extensive write-up from the app's publisher. This usually details its pertinent features, alongside details of what has been updated in the most recent version. Be sure to check the operating system requirements if you have an older iPad.

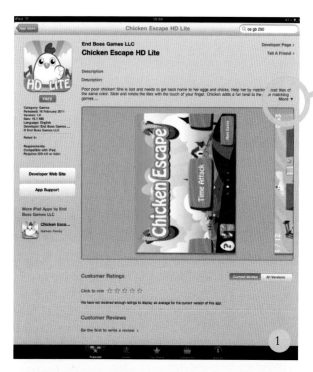

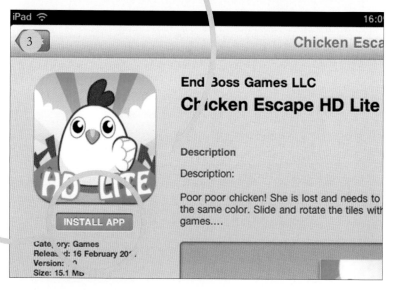

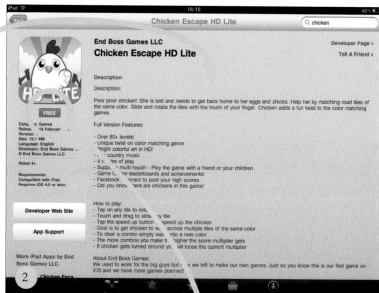

4. If you haven't installed any new apps or updates in the last few minutes, you'll be asked to confirm your password. This is to make sure that nobody is making unauthorised purchases with your account. You will receive an emailed receipt for all purchases that you do action a few days after you install them, with several totted up on a single invoice.

3. If you still want to download the app, click the button below its icon twice. This will read either *FREE*, or its price in the first instance, but tapping it for a second time changes these words to confirm that you want to install it.

How to keep your applications up to date

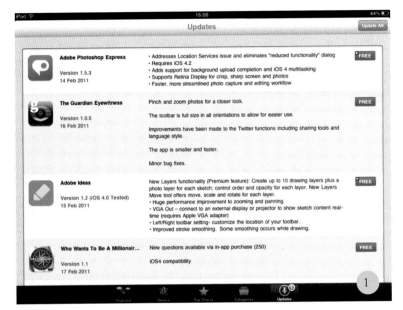

The iPad's active developer community is filled with enthusiastic coders who work tirelessly to keep their applications up to date, regularly shipping refreshed editions through the App Store. These updates are free to download, and you'll be notified when they are ready for you. Keep an eye on the App Store's icon on your iPad's home screen. When updates are ready it'll be overlaid by a small red badge, in the middle of which a number will tell you how many updates are ready to be shipped. If you don't see a badge, you're all up to date.

Open the App Store and tap the Updates icon at the end of the toolbar (again, this will have a badge attached, telling you how many updates are ready). This opens a page showing you what the updates are (*1*). You can install them one by one by tapping the button beside each one, or update all at once by tapping *Update All* at the top of the screen.

As your apps install their icon (*2*) or the folder holding them (*3*) will adopt a progress bar, showing you how long you still have to wait.

The *New* tab shows you the latest popular additions to the Store. This is the place to look if you're chasing featured new applications that you're unlikely to have seen before.

What's Hot shows you what people are downloading. Combine your investigations here with the *Top Charts*, accessible from the toolbar at the bottom of the interface.

Only interested in the very newest additions to the App Store? Tap *Release Date* to see which apps have just been released for sale and stay ahead of the crowd.

iBooks

The future of reading is almost certainly digital, and if Apple has any say in it the device through which you'll do that reading is the iPad or iPhone, using the iBooks application. What is it and how do you find books you want to read in its store?

i Books is an important application for the iPad. Apple is hoping that the iPad will become a book replacement, and that we'll choose to read books on a screen – specifically its own screen – rather than bound paper. It's not the first company to have this idea, as the likes of Sony (with the Reader) and Amazon (with the Kindle) already have competing products.

Your books are arranged on shelves, a little like the albums in the Music application. Tapping one opens it on the screen, either as a spread showing both the left and right pages on a landscape-oriented iPad, or as a single page on one held upright. Which you choose is up to you, but if your only reason for using it in portrait mode is that you can read it more easily because the text is larger, you may want to increase the font size.

This is managed through the font setting dialogue that hides behind the *AA* button at the top of each page (*see right*). Tap this and choose between smaller and larger characters in five common fonts. The button beside it – the picture of the sun – controls the brightness of the display so that you can tailor it to your eyes and the lighting conditions in which you're using your iPad.

On the far right of the toolbar is a magnifying glass, which calls up the search tool (*see far right, opposite page*). Tap this and enter your search term and it will hunt through the book you're reading to find every instance of that word combination. If it remains ambiguous or doesn't turn up a relevant answer, Google and Wikipedia buttons at the bottom of the results panel let you search online for more information.

Managing bookmarks and locations

Each time you open a book, iBooks will remember where you left it last time, so you shouldn't ever lose your place, and if you're on the contents page of a book you'll see a red resume tab at the top of the page, which when tapped takes you to your last-opened page. If you are reading the same book on several different devices, such as an iPad and an iPhone, your current position within the book will be synchronised between them.

You can set custom bookmarks throughout the text – a feature that will be particularly useful for academic texts. To set one, hold down on a word where you want to anchor it, and when you lift your finger you'll be presented with a short menu that lets you copy the

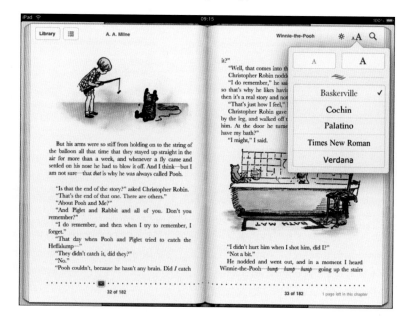

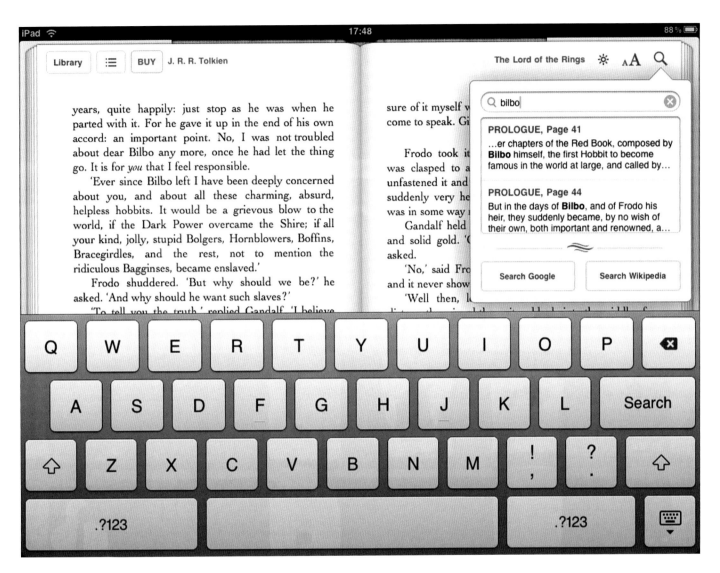

selected text, use it as a search term, look it up in the dictionary or set a bookmark (*see left*). Select the *Bookmark* option and the location will be saved in your bookmarks list, along with an excerpt and the date so that you can easily find it in the future. It's highly intuitive, and more use than a regular card marker in a printed book.

Fall in love with reading again

The longer you use iBooks, the more you'll fall in love with this way of reading, with a progress bar at the bottom of the screen showing how far through the book you've read, and the integrated dictionary helping make sure you're never lost in a sea of unfamiliar words. Together with the ease with which you can download new reading material, these features make static printed books feel very antiquated indeed.

How to buy a novel in iBooks

With iBooks, Apple has made it extremely easy to find and buy new books, by building its own iBookstore right into the application itself. You'll find it hiding behind the *Store* button on the toolbar that appears above your bookshelves. Here we'll walk through the process of downloading a sample from a book you might find interesting and then buying the complete volume using your iTunes Store account.

Tap iBooks' *Store* button to flip around the application like a secret passageway hidden behind a bookcase. On the back you'll find a store that closely resembles the App Store. Tap *Top Charts* to see what's selling well right now, and which are the most popular free books.

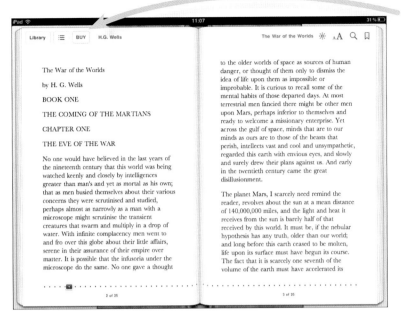

Enjoying the book? The *Buy* button appears at the top of each page in the sample, so even if you haven't finished reading through every page you've downloaded you can still buy the rest of the novel with a single tap. The Sample will stay in your library.

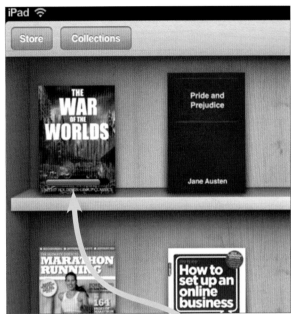

Tap *Get Sample* and a generous excerpt of your chosen book will be download to your iPad and deposited on your bookshelves. You can monitor the progress of the download by keeping an eye on the blue bar. When it has completed it will be strapped by the word '*Sample*' so you know it's not the full book. Tap the cover to look inside.

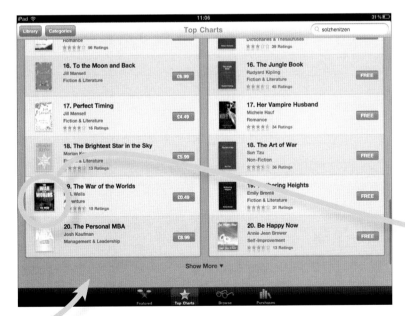

Scroll through the charts to find a book that grabs your interest. There are plenty to choose from, in all genres, but if nothing here takes your fancy use the search box at the top to hunt out a particular read.

Every full book is accompanied by an excerpt, which is free to download. This is the digital equivalent of flicking through a book on the shelves in you local bookshop, as it allows you to try it out before you buy the whole thing. The length of the excerpt varies between books, but should always be enough to give you a flavour of the full download.

Dictation

Save yourself a lot of time and effort by speaking to your iPad and letting it transcribe your words into lines of accurately recognised text. It's only for the 'new' iPad, but there are third-party solutions for those who have yet to upgrade.

Dictation is a core feature of the new iPad and a great reason to upgrade from the iPad 2 or original model, so it may surprise you to discover that it isn't enabled by default.

There's a very good reason for this, though: Dictation requires an active network connection so that it can send data back to Apple's servers for processing before feeding back the results as written text. As such, then, it's not a local feature, and Apple needs to be sure that you're happy for it to share this information with its servers.

As well as sending your live dictation, though, it also sends various items of data from your iPad applications so that it can personalise the experience by making it more effective at recognising family members, work

What data does Apple collect?

As stated in the Dictation feature privacy notice: '*When you use the keyboard dictation feature on your device, the things you dictate will be recorded and sent to Apple to convert what you say into text. Your device will also send Apple other information, such as your first name and nickname; the names, nicknames, and relationship with you (e.g., "my dad") of your address book contacts; and song names in your collection (collectively, your "User Data"). All of this data is used to help the dictation feature understand you better and recognise what you say. It is not linked to other data that Apple may have from your use of other Apple services.*'

contacts, yourself, the tracks you have in your Music library, and so on. Apple makes it clear that it doesn't tie this data to anything else it knows about you, so you shouldn't have any security worries here, but if you do then you don't have to enable the feature.

Enabling Dictation

The Dictation feature is considered an alternative keyboard by iOS. It is therefore controlled by the Keyboards section of the Settings application.

Open Settings and tap *General | Keyboard* and then tap the *ON / OFF* slider beside Dictation to turn it on. You'll be asked to confirm that you want to enable it. You should only do this if you're happy with the privacy terms and conditions, so if you've not yet read them step back to the settings screen and tap the *About Dictation and Privacy* link to call up the policy.

Dictation will now be active, so you can close the settings application and switch to whichever app you need to use it in.

Using Dictation

Think of Dictation as your long-lost shorthand secretary. Few businesses can afford to assign a secretary to each of their top staff any more, never mind their regular employees, but with features like Dictation the days of us all typing our letters personally could well be numbered, allowing us to kick back and just talk.

Where Dictation differs from a trusty secretary, though, is that it relies upon being told everything you want it to say – explicitly. So, don't assume that it knows where to put a full stop, comma or question mark; you have to tell it.

You don't need to speak particularly slowly, but you must speak clearly, pronounce your words properly and be specific about where your punctuation should appear. To dictate the previous sentence, you'd press the microphone button on the keyboard and say:

'You don't need to speak particularly slowly comma but you must speak clearly comma pronounce your words properly and be specific about where your punctuation should appear period'

Note that you don't need to explain where apostrophes should be used to contracted words such as 'don't'.

Dictation works with all iPad applications that take keyboard input, so you should also get into the habit of telling it how to lay out your text in the editing window. Clearly if you're working in an advanced layout app like Pages you can't use it to explicitly place text boxes, picture frames and so on, but taking the time to specify simpler layout commands such as '*new paragraph*', '*new line*' and so on will save you going back later on to break up long tracts of dictated text.

Dictation limitations

Dictation is a great feature, but at present it doesn't work in real-time. To do that it would need to process all of your transcriptions locally. This would require that it maintained an extensive underlying database of sound files against which to compare your spoken words. As a result, if you don't have a data connection you won't be able to use it.

Further, because all of the transcriptions are delivered retrospectively after they have been processed by the remote server you can't go back and change them quickly using voice commands in the same way you can when using many dictation tools on your Mac or PC. Instead you need to perform some tap-and-select intervention.

Perhaps most seriously, though, although Dictation is part of iOS 5.1, it only works on the iPhone 4S and new iPad. Anyone with an older model is locked out.

Fortunately there are alternatives, with third-party developers producing their own dictation apps for those who have yet to upgrade to the latest hardware. Dragon Dictation (*below*) is a free download from *bit.ly/ACoBNL*.

Like the native Dictation tool, this sends your spoken words to a remote server for transcription, with the results returned to your iPad in a matter of seconds. These can then be copied to another application or, with one tap, dropped into an email.

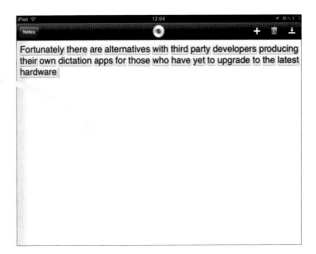

Alternatives to iTunes and iBookstore

What would the iPad be without great applications and first-rate content to use with it? The Internet is fit to burst with high quality media, much of which can be yours for free... legally.

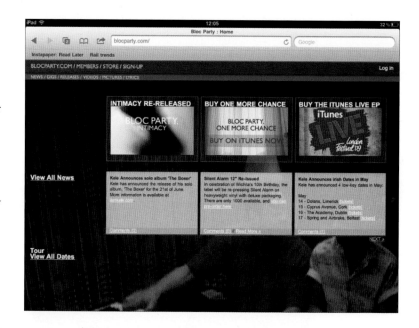

N ow that you've bought and set up your iPad, it's time to find some content to enjoy on it. The easiest way to do this is to buy from the iTunes Store, which offers music, movies and TV shows from around the world. However, there are often cheaper – and sometimes completely free – alternatives close at hand, as we'll show you here.

Music

Before the iTunes Music Store came along, it was practically impossible to legally download music: the major record companies simply didn't make it available. Out of that frustration grew alternatives such as the original Napster sharing service, which allowed you to freely (but illegally) swap your music collection with other users across the Internet.

Naturally, the record companies didn't like this much, and so they took legal action, ending the era of free-for-all downloading. Then came Apple's store, offering music from major artists for less than the price of the CD version. Now also offering TV series' and podcasts, it's still one of the best ways of filling up your iPad, with over half of UK music downloads now coming from here alone.

Although the original Napster is long gone, replaced by a legally compliant store of the same name, it's still possible to find plenty of free media online, legally, and without having to install complex programs. You may have to hunt around a little, but there are all sorts of hidden gems just waiting to be discovered – here's the inside track.

Artist homepages

If there's a particular artist that you're fond of, take a good look around their official website, which you should find easily enough through a search engine such as Google (*google.co.uk*). You can often hear a low-quality streaming version of their music, but you might also come across anything from promo videos and interviews, to MP3 files that you can save into your iTunes folder and transfer to your iPad.

You may also have to register first, by giving your email address and providing a username, but it's worth persevering to get to the 'inner sanctum' of these sites. It's often the first place you'll find previews of a new

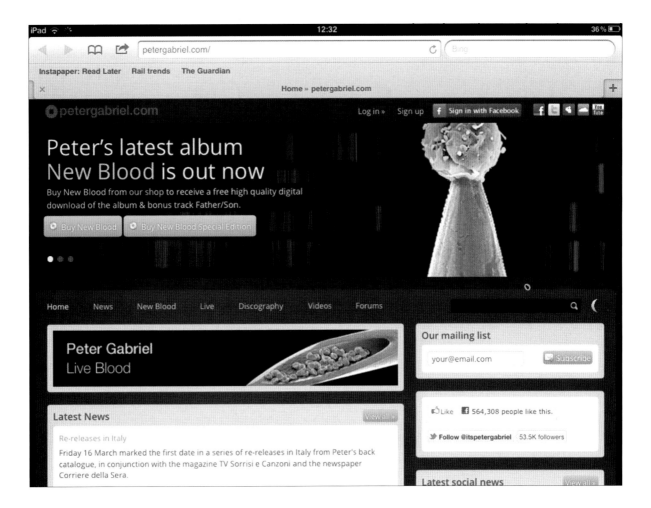

single, and it's also a great way to get hold of exclusive, previously unheard or live material. A browse around the Internet reveals all kinds of free downloads.

Bloc Party *blocparty.com*
Live, studio and demo tracks from the music press darlings of 2005. Also links to 'The Marshals' fan site, which offers further, unreleased material.

Elvis Costello *elviscostello.com*
Audio interviews in WMA format, where the master songsmith discusses his approach to writing. iTunes is capable of converting WMA tracks to iPod friendly formats.

Jamie Cullum *jamiecullum.com*
Jazz pianist, singer and BBC Radio 2 specialist music presenter's homepage, offering unreleased live tracks.

Peter Gabriel *petergabriel.com*
Previews and streamed listening abounds.

Sigur Ròs *sigur-ros.co.uk*
A generous selection of unreleased live and studio tracks from the site of the Icelandic shoe-gazers.

Record companies

With the Internet's potential to promote and distribute music, record companies are feeling more nervous than ever about their role. As such, many are recasting themselves as front-line champions of new music, as well as guardians of their artists' back catalogues.

Matador Records *matadorrecords.com*
From the label that houses indie-alternative notaries such as Interpol and Cat Power, a fine collection of unreleased

and new artist tracks. Follow the links on the front page for new album teaser tracks in their entirety, as well as videos of interviews and live performances.

Subpop *subpop.com*
Indie label with names such as Nirvana, The Afghan Whigs and Saint Etienne on its books. The Media link will take you to a page offering free downloads of individual tracks from established artists, as well as new signings. You can also subscribe to podcasts, which can be set to automatically download into iTunes when they're updated.

Rykodisc *rykodisc.com*
Long-running label with an extensive high-profile back catalogue. Go to the See and Hear Music section to find free artist-themed Podcasts, including some excellent interviews and album previews.

Victory Records *victoryrecords.com*
US-based rock label with a sizeable collection of good-quality MP3 downloads and streams in the Media section.

Kill Rock Stars *killrockstars.com*
A US label that has nurtured alternative folk heroes such as Elliot Smith and The Decemberists. Scroll down the page for a substantial archive of free music and video downloads.

Unsigned artists

It's not just signed artists who are keen to have you cramming their music onto your iPad. The Internet was hailed as a revolution for unsigned bands, as it took the means of distribution away from the major labels and put

it into the hands of the public. This has worked out well for the artists, and even better for the music enthusiast: a few leisurely clicks of your mouse can put you in touch with bands on the other side of the world. With so much competition out there, artists are also less precious about charging for their labours and many are happy to give away their music for the price of a listen – particularly if it might promote the later sale of an album or some concert tickets.

If you're feeling adventurous, we would recommend you start by heading to music-related online communities, where you'll find the homepages of countless artists looking for your attention.

Alternatively, there are more formalised sites that offer editorial content to help you narrow down the choice to your own tastes. Ultimately, there's no quality control other than your own ears, but that's all part of the attraction.

MySpace *myspace.com*
A general-interest online community and social-networking site, but with a particularly good music section. A good touch is the built-in music player that kicks in as soon as you land on a homepage. If you like what you hear, download the track. If not, move on. Not all artists will let you download full versions of their tracks, but the number of signed bands who have a presence here is an encouraging sign.

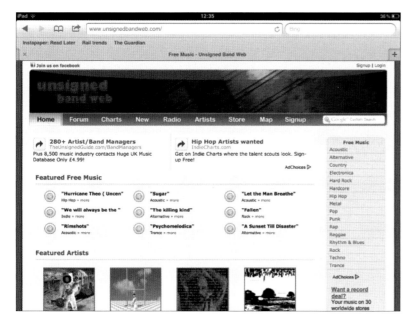

Unsigned Band *unsignedbandweb.com*
Another welcoming community for those artists
and bands looking for an audience. Some slightly rough
edges to the site are made up for by a choice of several
streaming web-based radio stations showcasing new
talent, active forums and a broad selection of genres.

Review sites

You don't have to rely on Rolling Stone or NME to get
your music news any more. There's a whole wealth of
online review sites, music magazines and blogs competing
for your attention, many of which also have links to free

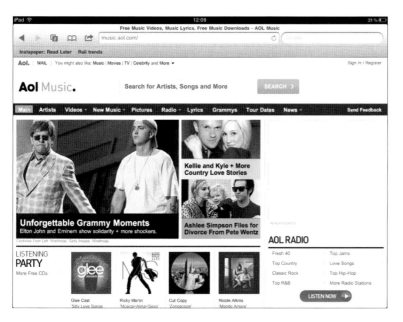

music. Subscribe to their feeds to keep an eye on what
they have on offer.

Epitonic *epitonic.com*
Describing itself as 'your source of cutting-edge music',
this magazine site offers a healthy complement of
editorial, as well as a whole stack of high-quality
downloads. There's also the Black Box feature, which
allows you to log in and play your favourite tracks from
anywhere. Mainly contemporary material.

Pitchfork Media *pitchforkmedia.com*
A review site aimed at picking out the crop of current
releases, dwelling mostly on urban, alternative and
indie-rock. The editorial and free MP3 downloads are
variable in quality, but it's up to date and rarely sits on
the fence.

Into Music *intomusic.co.uk*
An excellent combination of music magazine and
download service. There are nominal fees to gain access
to the music of signed bands, but many of the lesser-
known and unsigned artists are offering free downloads.

PeopleSound *www.peoplesound.com*
Combining signed and unsigned artists. Once you've
registered, you can download or stream from thousands
of tracks, as well as build up playlists of your favourites
that can be accessed and listened to from any computer.

Classic Cat *classiccat.net*
An exhaustive catalogue of links to freely downloadable
classical music, organised by composer. It can take a
while to navigate to external sites to actually download
the tracks, but it's worth it for the sheer amount of
music on offer.

Music stores

Amazon *amazon.com*
It may seem an odd gesture for the online retailing giant
to give away its goods, but that's what it's currently doing
with album tracks from featured artists, as well as

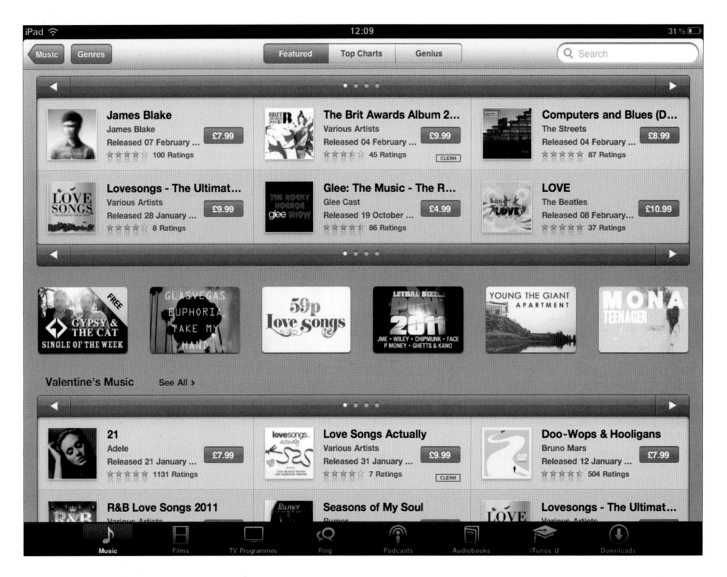

lesser-known music. Make sure you're using the US (.com) version of the site and follow the 'free downloads' link hiding on the top right of the Music section, then log in to download the MP3s.

Last.fm *http://last.fm*
Stream tracks from your favourite artists, along with those artists that complement your existing listening tastes from this seemingly inexhaustible library. It's a great way to discover new music and enrich your listening experience.

AOL *http://music.aol.com*
Dozens of free downloads from high-profile contemporary artists. Just be aware that when you download a track, the email address you provide is passed

on to the band's record company (although it's easily fooled), and you'll be automatically signed up for the AOL newsletter, too. Go to the Songs menu to find the download links.

iTunes Store
Not to be left out, even Apple's own store offers free downloads. These can generally be found advertised around the middle of the store's front page, and are generally updated every Tuesday. They also appear on the iPad version, again roughly half way down the page.

It's also worth signing up for updates from Apple and other outlets to be kept abreast of new content appearing on their stores, and keep an eye out for other freebies, including TV shows and, at Christmas, 12 days' worth of apps, music, movies and books.

Public domain

Under current UK law, the copyright on a piece of music lasts 70 years from the end of the year of the author's death, and 50 years for the recording itself. After that, copyright ceases, and it passes in to the public domain. So, a recording of Mozart's *Requiem Mass* recorded last year will still be under copyright, but one recorded in 1935 or before won't be.

The BBC used this to good effect with its Beethoven season in 2005, offering free downloads on its website, followed by a similar season of Bach. Using music recorded by its own orchestra, it could forgo paying extra royalties. More of these are planned in the future, so keep an eye on *bbc.co.uk/music*.

Naturally, it's generally older and mostly classical music that's going to be available in this way, but as major libraries around the world begin to put their archives online, expect to find all sorts of interesting examples appearing.

Public Domain 4 U *http://publicdomain4u.com*

A fascinating archive of public domain music, with a strong focus on early 20th century roots music, and no need to register.

The Piano Society *pianosociety.com*

A site for professional and amateur pianists to showcase their talent, the best are picked and given away as free MP3s. More than 50 classical composers are represented,

making this a great way to find high-quality and well-recorded piano music. There is also plenty of educational information about both the track and its author.

Creative Commons *http://creativecommons.org/*

Creative Commons is a relatively new form of copyright declaration that allows artists to prescribe exactly what can and can't be done with their online creations. There are six basic types of licence, plus more specialised versions, but most allow the download of work, at least for personal use. Go to *http://creativecommons.org/wired* to find an entire album of high-profile artists who got together with Wired magazine to produce an album that can be used for anything except advertising other products. There's also a special Google search engine built into the site, so you can scour the rest of the Internet for Creative Commons licensed works.

CCMixter *http://ccmixter.org*

This site hosts a huge number of samples and remixes derived from work licensed under the Creative Commons licensing scheme, which are themselves subject to the same copyright freedoms. Submission is open to all, but the quality is nonetheless excellent – a great example of how the scheme is changing music distribution.

Free Kids Music *http://freekidsmusic.com*

An American site offering music geared towards children. It's not all of great artistic merit, and contains a lot of links to adverts, but you'll find enough here to keep the kids amused for a while.

Books

Of course, it's not just music that you can find for free online. The App Store is fit to burst with free applications and, if you know where to look, there are plenty of free books on the net, too. To save you the chore of hunting them down, here is a selection of the best.

Project Gutenberg *http://gutenberg.org*

Project Gutenberg has long been the first place to turn if you want to download free books. It was established in 1971 by Michael Hart with the aim of digitising the 10,000 most consulted books and making them available to the public at little or no charge at all.

The first document to be digitised was the United States declaration of Independence, which has now been joined by over 34,000 other books and documents.

A non-profit corporation, Project Gutenberg is US-based, but its content is global in scope. On average 50 new e-books are added to its library each week, so even if the volume you'd like to read isn't yet there, there's a chance it could be soon. Neither is Project Gutenberg a purely English-language enterprise, with French, German, Finish, Dutch, Portuguese and Chinese particularly well represented.

Don't go there expecting to download the latest Jilly Cooper or the Steig Larsson *Millennium* trilogy any time soon: all books included in the archive are out of copyright, and so you won't find modern titles among them. However, if you feel the need to catch up with the classics then you will find an extensive selection to pick from, and for students it could prove a boon as it'll help reduce the cost of a full set of literature set texts. Just be aware of the fact that as you won't be reading from the same paper-based copy as your classmates, you won't reference the same page numbers.

Subscription services

The Internet has caused all sorts of headaches for those concerned with intellectual property, but it's even more confusing for the consumer. There was a time when you bought a CD and could pretty much do whatever you wanted with it, but the album you've just bought from the Internet doesn't physically exist.

That's led to a new model of subscription services, whereby for a set amount of money each month you can effectively 'rent' a music collection, which you lose the right to play should you cancel your subscription. Sadly, although it has been adopted by high-profile names including Napster, HMV and Virgin, none of these services are compatible with the iPad – something that's not clear until you trawl through the small print. Apple itself has in the past publicly said it has no plans to offer such a service.

There are, however, a couple of companies that allow you to download tracks for a set monthly fee. If you buy more than an album or two a month, even from iTunes, these services can work out a lot cheaper.

Wippit *wippit.com*

Wippit has 600,000 recordings from 200 record labels, and also has a hefty classical music section, as well as a free downloads area for non-subscribers.

You'll then get unlimited access to the library, which is regularly rotated, so you're guaranteed a fresh supply. All the other music on the site is available at a discounted 'subscribers rate', which varies by track. Unfortunately, there's not a huge amount currently available in an iPad-compatible MP3 format, so to avoid disappointment, make sure you use the advanced filter to only show these.

eMusic *emusic.com*

Going to the homepage of this subscription site it will immediately ask you to subscribe – even the 14-day free trial requires you to enter your credit card details before you get any more information. Don't let that put you off, though – you can bypass this to check out the site by going directly to *emusic.com/browse/all.html*. You can also cancel your subscription before the end of the free period. If you do, not only will you not be charged, but you'll also be able to keep any tracks you've downloaded.

Three levels of monthly subscription are available. There's no minimum sign-up period, and you can keep the tracks if your subscription lapses. A great-value option.

Spotify *spotify.com*

The current darling of streamed music services offers a subscription service that allows you to download tracks to a portable player and also streams its massive library without the frequent ads that interrupt the listening experience of non-paying users.

It's now available in the US, but is unavailable around much of the rest of the world outside Europe, currently at least.

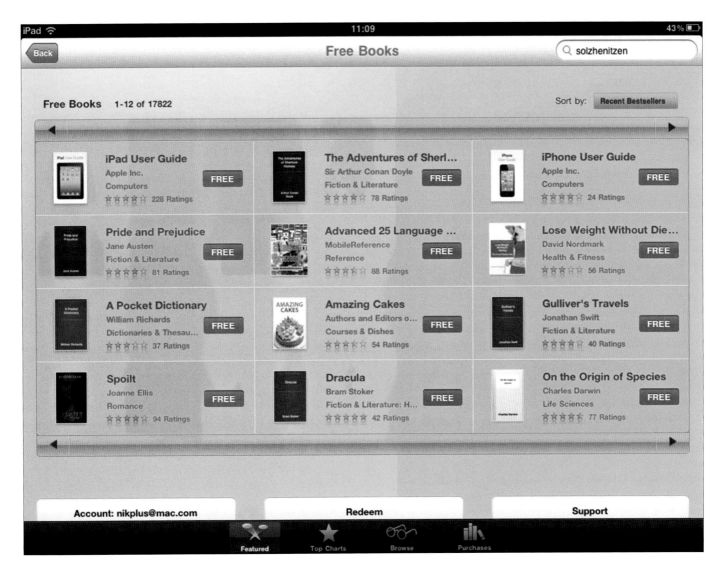

The project is largely run by volunteers, who work on titles of interest to them and post them to the site. Over the years, the range of formats in which books have been available has grown, from plain text and HTML to now include ePub both with and without images, Kindle format, again with and without images, Plucker and QiOO Mobile. If you're downloading books to read on your iPad, opt for one of the two ePub formats as these can be handled natively by the iBooks app.

You are free to pass on any of the books that you download from Project Gutenberg, and those to whom you give them can also do the same, as the project's goal extends to making electronic books as widely available as possible.

The best place to start looking for a book to read is the 100 most popular downloads. Visit *gutenberg.org* and click

Top downloads on the bar that runs across the top of the page. This will initially present you with a list of the top 100 downloads from the previous day, but scrolling further down the page also pulls up lists of the top 100 authors, the top 100 downloads of the last seven days and of the last 30 days.

These charts often exhibit a very populist trend, with titles such as *The Adventures of Huckleberry Finn* by Mark Twain, *The Adventures of Sherlock Holmes* by Sir Arthur Conan Doyle, *Pride and Prejudice* by Jane Austen and *A Tale of Two Cities* by Charles Dickens featuring regularly.

Project Gutenberg is not only an excellent free online resource that greatly reduces the cost of building an iPad library, but also a great way for students and anyone who would care to better themselves to catch up on the classics they may have missed.

Apple iBook store

Many of the classics available through Project Gutenberg also appear on Apple's own iBook store, which is accessed by tapping Store button at the top of the iBooks application. As with the App Store, Apple maintains download charts for both paid and free content.

Tap Top Charts on the toolbar at the bottom of the iBooks application to find them, and look in the right-hand column for the free downloads.

One of the most popular books of all time on the store is *Winnie the Pooh*, which is an excellent example of how books should be done due to its well handled graphics and text. However it's just one of thousands of ePub titles available on the store. Be aware, though, that the quality of free books available is more varied than that of commercial options. It pays to check out reviews and ratings to see how other readers have judged the quality of the finished product. Find a good one, though, and like the titles served by Project Gutenberg, it's a cost-effective way to expand your knowledge of the classics.

Kindle

Amazon clearly understood the importance of selling books through as many platforms as it could, and so as well as producing its own hardware e-book reader, called Kindle, it has created a software version of the same name which runs on the iPad, iPhone, iPod touch and other handheld devices. Early iterations of this software let you buy books directly from the front screen, but since Apple changed the terms under which it agrees to serve

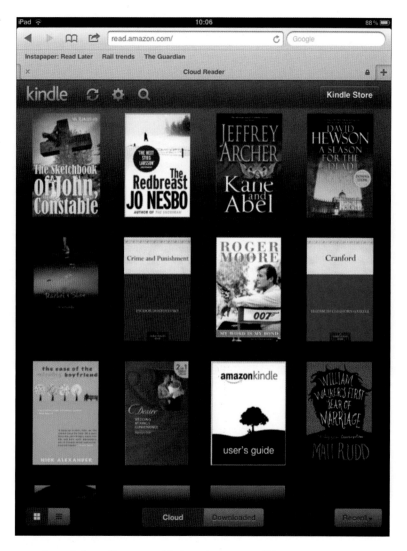

apps through its online store this is no longer possible, as Amazon would have been forced to hand over 30% of the price of each download. As it generally pays publishers of the highest value books it sells royalties of 70%, handing over the remaining 30% to Apple would have wiped out its profits entirely.

Fortunately it came up with an answer, which is a dedicated online cloud edition of the Kindle software, hosted at *read.amazon.com* (*left*).

This gives you access to any books you've already bought from its store and, crucially, a direct link to the Kindle Store from which you can stock up on new reading material.

Internet Archive *http://archive.org*

The Internet Archive, at *archive.org*, is more often associated with storing archived copies of websites for future posterity. However, the *Texts* section, which is accessed from the menu at the very top of the page, is also home to a range of more than two and a half million e-books and electronic texts.

Helpfully, these are subdivided into smaller collections, including dedicated American and Canadian libraries, Universal Library and a children's library. You will find a considerable overlap with Project Gutenberg here, but it is still worth keeping an eye on for those titles that do not appear in the Gutenberg archive.

Open Library *http://openlibrary.org*

Open library has set itself what it calls a 'lofty but achievable goal'. It wants to create a single web page for every book ever published, and to date has gathered more than 20 million records towards the accomplishment of that goal. It works much like Wikipedia as a collaborative

project to which anyone can create, add or correct records within its database.

Of greatest interest, though, is its collection of e-books, which can be found by typing a title into the search box found at the top of each page and checking the box beside 'Only show ebooks'.

The results it throws up are impressive. The search for *Pride and Prejudice*, for example, brought up 753 editions of Jane Austen's work, including *Mansfield Park*, *Northanger Abbey*, *Emma*, and of course *Pride and Prejudice*. Where available as physical books there are links to buy or borrow them as appropriate, and the options for reading electronic versions are extensive. They include PDF and plain text, and two formats for iPad reading. The ePub links download versions that are compatible with the iPad's iBooks app, and a Send to Kindle option takes you back to Amazon's own website where you can choose the device that should receive the downloaded file.

Why won't my music download?

Unfortunately, there's no standard way of streaming or downloading music from a website, so you need to be selective in the formats that you download from free online libraries. One of the most common formats, MP3, is compatible with iPads, and iTunes will also convert most other formats, such as WMA files.

If you have iTunes installed, you'll have Apple's Quicktime player, too. This becomes the default player for various types of streamed media, but will usually treat any MP3 download as a stream too, preventing its

download. To get around this, load Quicktime and open its application Preferences. On the File Types tab, uncheck the boxes marked 'Streaming Audio'.

Depending on what else is installed on your PC, there may be other programs that take over when you click on a download link – RealPlayer, WinAMP and Windows Media Player, for example. If that happens, look for an option in the program to save the current media. If there isn't one, close the program, go back to the link, and right-click on it. If a Save Target As option appears, you can use this to download the MP3 file directly to your computer.

Chapter 3
iPad workshops

Twitter

The world's most popular online messaging service is built into the very heart of iOS 5, allowing you to Tweet directly not only from the Twitter application, but from several core iPad apps, too.

T witter, the web-based messaging system that has taken the world by storm, is now a core feature of iOS 5 on the iPhone and iPad. It's built in at the heart of the operating system, making it easier than ever to send short links and notes to your friends directly from inside some of the most important preinstalled applications.

Signing in to Twitter on your iPad

1. Tap *Settings | Twitter* to open the Twitter settings application and then start the process by tapping *Add Account* and entering your details. You can't actually sign up to Twitter through the Settings app. If you don't already have an account, sign up at *twitter.com*.

2. Allow your iPad to add Twitter contacts to the records in Contacts. It does this by comparing your contacts' details with records already assigned to Twitter accounts and adding the Twitter usernames to any matching cards that it finds.

3. Although it looks like only the Twitter app can post to your account from your iPad, Twitter is actually built in to a number of the core iOS applications, including Photos and Maps, the latter allowing you to 'check in' at a location so your friends know where you are. While you can explicitly turn off these extra features on the iPhone and iPod touch, the only service you can deactivate on the iPad is vanilla Twitter posting. If you want to do this, tap the *ON* slider at the bottom of the settings screen.

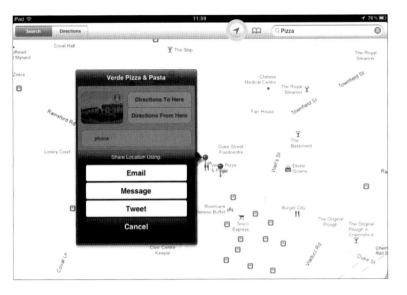

Either connect to a wifi network or, if you have a 3G- or 4G-enabled iPad, connect to the cellular network, and find your current location in Maps by tapping the location button on the toolbar (circled, *left*). After a second or two it will pinpoint your location and drop a pushpin to show where you are. Tap this to call up the geographic details, followed by *Share*.

You have a choice of three methods for sharing your location including email, message and tweet. It's the last of these that interests us here. Tap it to update your current location to a new message that you can either send to the Twitter community en masse, or share just with friends and specific contacts by sending a direct message (*see p78*).

It goes without saying that you should be careful about how much information of this sort you share with the general public. Anyone who knows where you live may know that your house is empty if you tweet a distant location. This could encourage burglary, and upset your insurance company.

Checking in with Twitter

If you're one of the many Twitter users who likes to check in everywhere you go and let your friends know where you are, there's no need to manually type in your address details any more.

Tweeting from YouTube

How often have you watched an amusing video on YouTube and immediately emailed a link out to your friends? It's much easier to do the same thing over Twitter – particularly as you can now do it directly from the iOS YouTube application.

Make sure the video isn't playing in full screen either by turning your iPad to portrait orientation or by tapping the double-ended arrow icon in the bottom right corner to shrink it down into the YouTube app control interface.

Now tap the video itself, followed by the Share icon that overlays it on a semi-transparent band at the top of the image (*above left*). From this, select *Tweet* and it will be clipped to a new Twitter message (*above right*), ready to be sent out to your followers.

Although you might imagine from the interface that this sends the video as an attached file, it doesn't – it simply sends a shortened address which, when clicked, sends your followers to the original on YouTube.

Finding friends and contacts

When we set up our Twitter account in iOS, we authorised it to interrogate our Contacts app to see how many of our friends and family had also signed up to Twitter using email addresses that we already knew. This allows the iPad to search these details and use them alongside the list of people we follow on Twitter to help address new direct messages and mentions.

To specifically draw another Twitter user's attention to something you're posting you need to 'mention' them. This is done by tapping the @ symbol at the start of the message and then entering their name (*1*). As you continue typing, the Twitter tools refine the list of results, narrowing down the possible number of people you might be wanting to talk to until it comes down to the exact result you're after (*2*). If you can see the person you want in the shortlist before this point, you can tap their name to select it.

The default action here is for Twitter to format the username as a mention, which is to say that while whatever you send will appear in their activity panel and be emailed to them to draw their attention to it, it will also appear in the public timeline so that it can be seen both by other Twitter users and by anyone else on the web. This is signified by the fact that the original @ you entered is still attached to the front of the targeted username (*3*).

If you want to send your tweet privately so that it can only be read by the recipient, you need to convert it to a Direct Message by swapping out the @ for a D, followed by a space (*4*). D, here, stands for Direct.

Bear in mind that while Twitter has high standards of privacy and that nothing you send with a D prefix will appear in anyone else's timeline, there is a possibility that the content of your private tweet may have to be divulged to law enforcement authorities around the world should they serve Twitter with the necessary papers to force it to do so.

If you have more than one Twitter account – perhaps one personal account and one professional one – you can add both of them to iOS 5 and switch between them. With two or more accounts in place, you'll see a new *From:* line at the top of the tweet card (*5*). To switch to your alternative account, tap this and select the account you want from the drop-down menu.

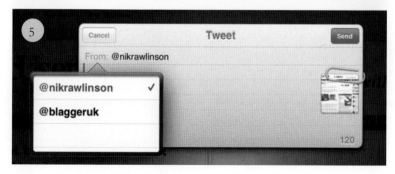

Tweeting a web link

In much the same way that Twitter can help you share links to videos you have enjoyed on YouTube, it also lets you send links of regular web pages to your followers without having to address them directly by email.

The option to tweet a web page is found on the menu that drops down from the shortcut button on the Safari toolbar, along with printing the page contents and the option to add a link to your iPad home screen.

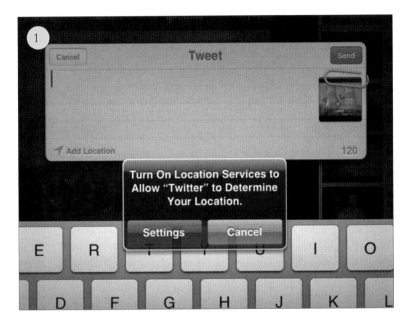

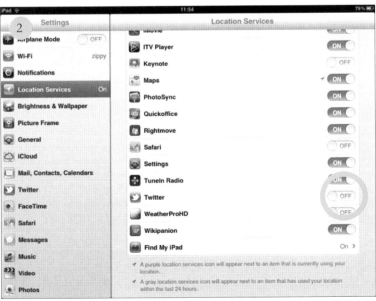

Twitter and your location

We have already covered off sharing your location over Twitter from the iOS Maps app. However, no application can share your location unless you specifically authorise it to do so.

All of the iOS Location Services are organised through the Preferences app. Although you can go there manually and authorise every application on your iPad, you don't need to do so until you need to use the service for each app. When you do, iOS will flash up an alert directing you to authorise it (*1*).

To add your location to a tweet – particularly if you're tweeting a picture from the Photos app and want to tell people where it was taken – tap *Add Location* on the bottom of the tweet card, and if the warning pops up tap *Settings* to open Location Services.

Scroll down the list of installed applications until you find Twitter (they are organised alphabetically) and tap the *OFF / ON* slider to switch it on (*2*).

Why might you not want to keep Location Services active for all apps all the time? Because those that keep polling a remote server to update your location will both eat into your bundled data allowance that comes as part of any 3G or 4G contract, and run down your battery because it's keeping both the processor and communications system active at all times.

Fortunately Twitter doesn't constantly poll the server, but you can see when any application is using Location Services to track your position because the compass pointer will be displayed in the clock bar at the top of the iPad display. A purple icon will also be displayed beside its switch in the Location Services control panel.

Message Centre

In a move that has effectively silenced the parade of alerts that might otherwise bombard the average tablet user, Apple has introduced Message Centre, which keeps all notifications organised in one place.

As a constantly-connected mobile device, the iPad receives updates, alerts and notifications all the time... game updates, emails, iMessages, appointments; the list is never-ending.

If it was to flash up each one as soon as it arrived, you'd be forever acknowledging an incessant stream of dialogue, and it wouldn't be long before you considered your iPad not an assistant, but a pest.

That's why when Apple rolled out iOS 5 it introduced a brand new feature called Message Centre, which puts all of your alerts in one location, so you always know where to find them, and they aren't constantly interrupting you.

It's enabled by default; to find it, simply rest your finger on the clock at the top of the screen, in either portrait or landscape orientation, and drag down to slide out a hidden drawer containing all of the updates you've received so far (*above right*).

You'll notice that the updates are grouped together according to the application to which they relate, so that all of your appointments, for example, appear together in a calendar sub-group.

If you prefer you can change to a chronological list that orders your alerts according to when they were received, or re-organise the order in which the various named applications appear on the list.

To do this, tap *Settings | Notifications* where you'll find a list of all Message Centre-ready applications listed (*below left*). Tap the *Edit* button at the top of the screen to call up grab handles at the end of each application entry. These are blocks of horizontal lines, which when touched and dragged up and down the list move the selected application.

Opening each app's entry in turn gives you a further set of options for refining the way in which it works with

Message Centre. Crucially, from here you can remove it from Message Centre altogether by tapping the ON/OFF slider (*left*). If you turn it off, it will be removed from the primary list on the previous screen and tucked away at the bottom of the page alongside the other applications whose notifications aren't handled this way.

As well as appearing in Message Centre, activated applications will flash up a message on the screen as soon as the alert becomes active. You can disable this by choosing None as the alert style, but it's more useful to leave it set to *Banners* or *Alerts*. The first of these drops down the alert from the top of the screen, leaves it there for a couple of seconds and then takes it away automatically. The second – Alerts – flashes up a traditional alert box in the middle of the screen, which can only be dismissed by a tap. This is useful for more important alerts such as alarms and reminders, while you might leave game updates and incoming iMessages set to Banners.

It's up to you whether or not these appear in the lock screen. This is something you can set by tapping the *View in Lock Screen* slider, but bear in mind that if you've set a passcode to prevent anyone else from seeing things on your iPad by just picking it up, bear in mind that if you choose this option they may be able to read alerts that you would rather keep private.

Many applications can pop up significant numbers of alerts – the calendar application, for example, or Facebook if you have a busy account – in which case you may want to change the number of alerts that are shown in each section of the Message Centre drop-down by tapping *Show* and choosing from one, five, 10 or 20.

Reminders

Much more than a simple task manager, Reminders is all you need to keep on top of the jobs that need doing, and when they ought to be done. With multiple lists and a tally of completed jobs, it a great motivator, too.

Reminders is a deceptively simple application. At first glance it appears to be nothing more than a simple list taker, giving you somewhere to jot down thoughts and reminders so that you don't need to worry about forgetting them.

Dig deeper, though, and you'll see that it's actually far more accomplished. Reminders lets you set deadlines, among other things, by which your jobs must be completed. Here, we'll show you how.

How to set reminders

1. Fire up Reminders and start adding notes. Use the '+' button at the top of the interface to start work on your first one, and press Return at the end of entering each one. This immediately takes you to the next line so you can start entering the next one without tapping '+' again.

2. Let's start adding some deadlines. We'll tap the Back up computer task, followed by *Remind Me*, and then the ON/OFF slider beside *On a Day*, then use the tumblers to select a date and time by which the job must be done. There's a *Today* tumbler for anything urgent.

3. Backing up your computer is a very important job, so we'll give it a priority, too. Tap *Done* to return to the main settings tab, followed by *Show More* and *Priority*, then select *High* from the list of options.

4. Before we can back up our computer we need to make sure we have sufficient storage, so we'll buy a new hard

drive. We can remind ourselves that we need to do this without creating a whole new reminder on the main screen by tapping within the Notes field and tapping in our reminder.

We've completed the first step in building ourselves a working list of tasks. Tap *Done* to return to the overall Reminders list and you'll see that we have now set deadlines for the two jobs.

Organising your reminders

By default, Reminders organises your jobs according to the lists on which they appear. There are two pre-set lists: Completed and Reminders. At the moment the jobs we have set ourselves appear on the Reminders list.

Should you have a specific project that you are working on and you want to hive off the tasks related to just that job, tap *Edit* on the Reminders home screen, followed by *Create New List...* You can then switch between your two lists and keep your jobs separate from one another.

When you have completed one of your tasks, tap the check box beside its name on the reminder list, then tap the *Completed* list in the sidebar. You'll see that your accomplished job has been moved to this new list and, when you return to the original list it has disappeared. This lets you keep a track of what you have accomplished over time (5).

If you want to delete a completed task entirely, tap its entry on the Completed list, followed by the *Delete* button on the pop-out tab.

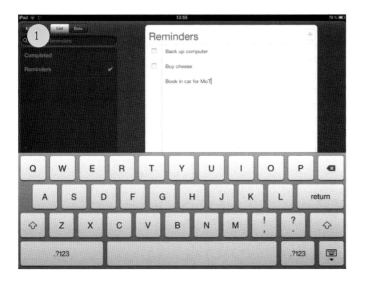

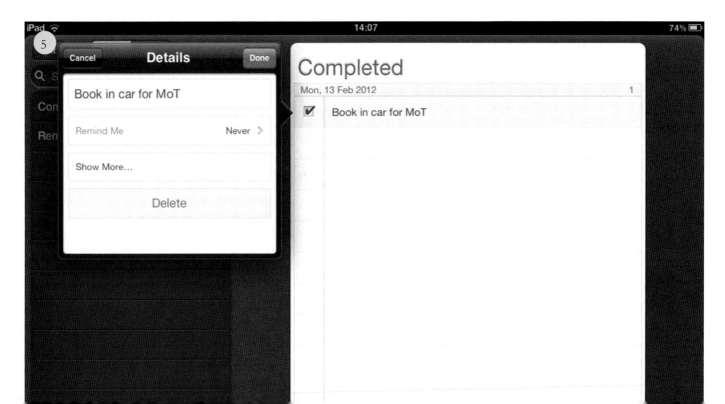

iMessage

With the introduction of iOS 5 Apple opened up its own mobile messaging system, iMessage, which lets you exchange messages with other iPad, iPhone, iPod touch and Mac users without paying carrier fees.

iMessage is Apple's proprietary messaging system, designed to be used as a supplement to regular text and picture messaging on devices running iOS 5 and later. In effect, it therefore adds a kind of text messaging feature to the iPod touch and iPad, neither of which had that functionality before, and supplements the regular multimedia and text messaging features that have long been a part of the iPhone's core set-up.

Setting up iMessage

Before you can use it, you must enable iMessage by tapping *Preferences | Messages*, and then tapping the OFF/ON switch to activate the service. By default it works with your Apple ID, which is the same address as you'll use to buy applications, music and books from Apple's various stores. You'll therefore need to type in your password to authorise the messaging service as an add-on to your ID's existing capabilities (*see grab 1, opposite page*).

Once up and running, scroll down to the *Receive At* box and tap it to see where messages can be received. When first set up, it will list only the email address associated with your Apple ID (on the iPhone it will also list your phone number). If you want to include another address at which people are more likely to find you, tap *Add Another Email...* and type it in (*2*).

The more email addresses you enter, the better, as it will increase the chances of your contacts being able to get in touch with you without having to specifically ask you what your iMessage username is. However, no matter how many you add, it will always default to displaying

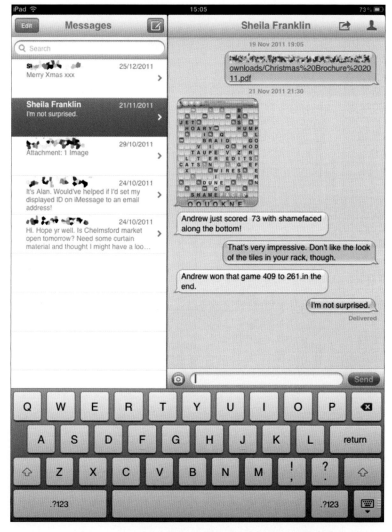

iMessage is smarter than the average messaging system, allowing you to exchange not only regular images and text, but also iOS screen grabs and hyperlinked web addresses.

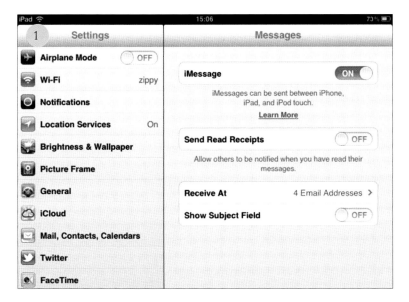

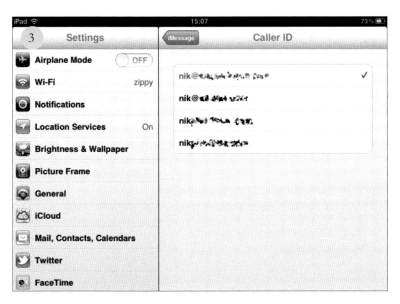

your Apple ID on outgoing messages. Apple calls this your Caller ID, showing how – on the iPhone, at least – the service has its roots in the traditional world of mobile phone text messaging.

You should take this opportunity to change the Caller ID (*3*) to either your main email address through which most people will be able to find you, so they aren't surprised to receive a message from an address they don't already know, or to an address that you don't mind handing out as a destination intended purely to handle iMessage traffic. For example, you might not want to use your Apple ID if that isn't an address that you routinely give out, as every iMessage that you send will automatically include it, thus giving it out to all of your contacts.

You can now step back through the iMessage screens to the opening panel and decide whether you want the option to include a subject field, and whether to send read reccipts to people who message you. We have left both of these switched off on our iPad (*grab 1 again*).

Why? Because while you might think differently we consider subject lines to be unnecessarily complex on a system that is set to rival text messaging, which by its very nature is a simplistic single-line medium. Further, we don't necessarily want people pestering us for answers to a message as soon as they know we have read it. If we had authorised it to send Read Receipts, our contacts would know instantly if we had seen their incoming message.

Using iMessage

You can now send iMessages directly by tapping on the Messages app on the home screen and typing in what you want to say, using your contact's email address as the destination, or through some of the other applications that form part of iOS 5.

For example, open an image from the Photos app and tap the shortcut button on the bottom toolbar (it looks like a curved arrow coming out of a rectangular box). Here you'll find an option for Message which, when tapped, drops your image into a new message with space above for you to write a covering note.

iMessages synchronise through your account so if you have several iOS devices you'll find the same message stream on each one of them.

Photo Stream

Apple has made it easy to share your photos and enjoy them on any device by introducing Photo Stream, which synchronises your shots between all of your iOS devices and backs them up to your Mac or PC.

The iPad has sported a camera since day one. So has the iPhone, while the iPod touch – the third product in Apple's line-up to run iOS – now also has one front and back. They're great for using FaceTime, of course, but for many of us the only real use for a camera is to take pictures of our family and friends.

Apple recognises this, which is why it's built in some rudimentary editing tools as part of iOS 5 and has always included an app for organising our images into groups, called Photos. It now also ships iPhoto for iOS.

The trouble is, with more of us than ever using our iPhones and iPads as cameras, we are finding ourselves connecting our devices to our Macs and PCs more often to download the results. That is contrary to what Apple has been trying to do with its iOS 5-and-later products, which is to produce entirely stand-alone devices that can be used without reference to a computer.

That's why it introduced Photo Stream. This simple idea works with an Apple ID to upload your 1000 most recently-taken images to Apple's servers, and from there synchronise them to all of your other iOS devices, so long as they're logged in to the same account. That 1000 photo limit is a cumulative number, shared by all of your devices, so in the unlikely event that you take 600 pictures one month on your iPhone you'll only have room for another 400 shot on your iPad before it starts to remove the oldest ones.

Even if you don't take 1000 pictures a month, any that are more than 30 days old will still expire from any devices to which they have been synchronised. Although the originals will be retained on whichever device originally shot them, it is important, therefore, to copy any that you want to keep on a synchronised device to its local library.

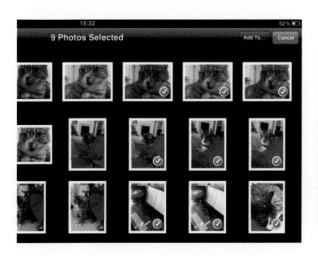

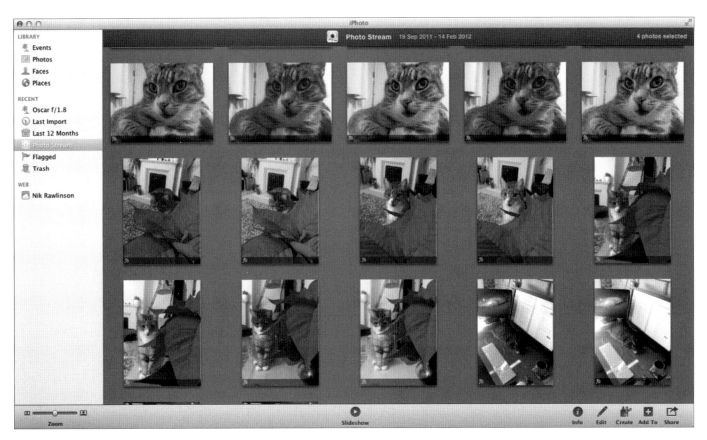

To do this on the iPad, open the Photos application and tap the *Photo Stream* button at the top of the screen. This shows you all of your synchronised photos. Tap the shortcut button (the curved arrow coming out of a box), followed by the photos you want to copy out of your Photo Stream. As you can see in the far left image on the opposite page, we have selected nine images, which have been checked with a blue tick. When you've finished selecting your pictures, tap *Add To...* and pick either *Add to Existing Album* or *Add to New Album*.

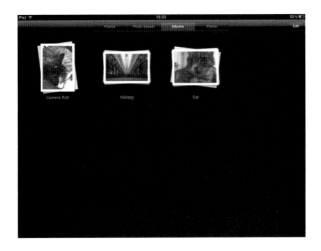

In our example, we've chosen to create a new album, which we've called Cat (*see facing page*). As soon as we tap *Save*, the album is created and the images copied to it (*below*). They still appear in the Photo Stream to indicate that they remain synchronised with other devices.

If you're a Mac user then you have another option for saving your synchronised images, which is to link either Aperture or iPhoto (*above*) to your account by selecting Photo Stream in the sidebar and entering your Apple ID and password. Every time you start the application it will check for updates to the Photo Stream and download any new additions to your library. Unlike any synchronised to an iOS device, these won't expire.

Windows PC users, for whom iPhoto isn't available, can also enjoy automatic backups by downloading and installing iCloud Control Panel from *apple.com/icloud/setup/pc.html*.

Open the control panel and click *Photo Stream*, followed by the ON/OFF slider to activate the service. Now open the regular Windows Control Panel and navigate to the iCloud settings. There, click the *Options* button beside the Photo Stream entry and select the local download and upload folders you want to use.

Pages

It may be unfamiliar to PC users, but Pages is a hit on the Mac. Now it's made the transition to the iPad, where it provides not only writing tools, but rudimentary page layout features, too.

P ages is a very accomplished word processor, giving you fine-grained control over the look of your work, with multiple fonts and the kind of layout options you might expect to find on your desktop.

It works well with the iPad's screen-based keyboard, but really flies when you marry it with an external keyboard – either by Bluetooth or using the Dock-connected keyboard that Apple sells as an optional extra. Dock it in portrait orientation and you'll have access to the formatting toolbar that runs across the top of the screen, with a comfortable, tactile keyboard below.

Pages is more than a simple text input application, though – it also has some pretty impressive layout tools at its disposal. The toolbar button sporting the framed mountain view is the media button, giving access to your photo library so you can insert pictures into your documents. There are further tools for creating tables, charts and shapes to illustrate your work.

Project Proposal

Impressively, for a device that doesn't have a mouse attached, once these elements are placed on your pages you have a lot of control over the way they look. Place a photo, for example, and you can drag it around the page with a finger and watch as your text re-flows around it. It will be positioned within a frame with grab handles at the corners. Dragging these with your finger changes the shape of the borderless box in which it sits, while double-tapping the graphic itself gives you access to a resizing tool. This is a simple slider that enlarges your picture when dragged to the right and makes it smaller when dragged to the left.

Pages has been written to work with other applications. The *My Documents* button at the top of the screen calls up a gallery of your work, and tools for creating new files, emailing those that already exist or exporting them in one of three formats: Pages, PDF and Word for use on a Mac or PC. This way you can use the mobile edition of Pages when you're away from home or the office, confident that you will have no problem continuing work on the same document when you return to base.

If you have signed up to Apple's online iCloud service, you can also synchronise each of your documents between all of the iOS devices on which you have installed iWork. Unfortunately it doesn't yet sync with a desktop or laptop Mac, but this may change with the next iWork update, and there are indications that Mac users will be able to more easily access documents they've created in the iOS edition when the Mac's operating system is updated to Mountain Lion in late summer 2012.

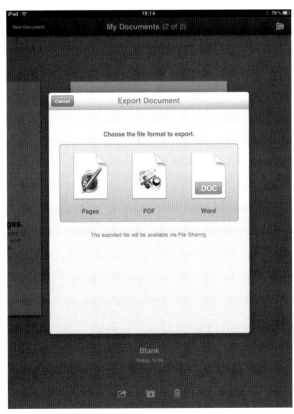

The many views of Pages

Above: The general editing view is dominated by your writing space. To the top of the screen is the formatting toolbar and ruler, both which can be hidden from view if you find them distracting. You can also hide the darker bar, which is where you need to look when inserting shapes and images, or skip out of the editing view and back to the document organiser.

Above right: Despite being a tablet-based word processor controlled by nothing more sophisticated than your fingers, Pages lets you perform surprisingly advanced editing tasks, including resizing images. We're doing that here using an overlaid slider dialogue.

Right: Although Pages has a preference for its own proprietary format, which works with Pages on the Mac, PC users and anyone who wants to share their documents will want to export in a different format.

Working with Pages

Pages is more than just a pretty face: it's a fully-featured word processor that gives you extensive control over styles and layouts. In fact, when paired with a printer and the iPad's built-in email app, it can be the bedrock of your mobile office.

Understanding the Pages interface

Documents	*Formatting*	*Styles*	*Media*	*Tools*
Tap to return to the file manager and create new documents.	Set font face, size, alignment and emphasis on a case-by-case basis.	Access pre-set styles, or tweak the current formatting.	Insert images, tables and shapes. Access your photo library.	Change document settings and margins, output to a shared printer and more

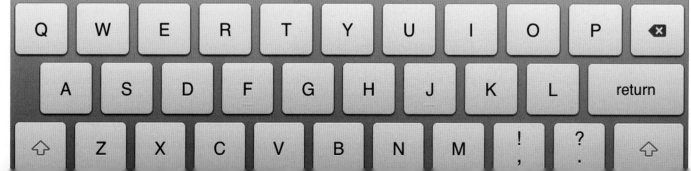

Setting up your document layout

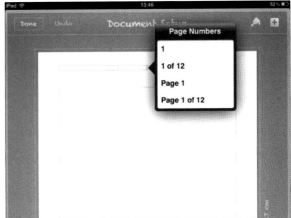

Pages is a very accomplished layout application, as we'll show you over the next few pages, but for most of the time the majority of users will simply want to type out notes, letters and essays on a plain sheet of paper.

It pays, therefore, to set up your document to meet your requirements before starting work. To do this, tap the spanner icon on the Pages toolbar and select *Document Setup*. Whichever way up you're holding your iPad it'll switch to portrait orientation at this point, with an outline of your document shown on blueprint paper.

Tap in the zones at the top and bottom of the page outline to set a header and footer if you want one. Each of them is split into three sections for left-, right- and centre-aligned content, and you can drag both these and the boundaries of the page text by using the grey arrows that appear above and below them (*above left*). You can drag the content margins in and out in the same way.

To add page numbers, tap the # icon on the toolbar and select the numbering type you need (*above right*). Tap *Done* when you've finished to return to you document.

Working with Styles

Like its desktop counterpart, the iOS edition of Pages uses the concept of Styles for formatting text in your documents. Styles are collections of text attributes, such as the font face and character size, that can be applied with a single tap, ensuring that you're consistent throughout your document by keeping all of your headings, body copy, titles and so on in line.

Although you can still format text bit by bit, by selecting fonts, sizes and emphases from the toolbar, it quickly pays dividends to get into the habit of working with styles instead, if for no other reason than the fact that you'll get more done in less time.

Styles are found in the dropdown menu accessed by tapping '*i*' on the toolbar. Tap the *Style* button here and then scroll down to the *Paragraph Style* section where you'll find the styles set as part of your chosen template.

It's not possible to change the predefined styles in the templates, but you can import documents created on a Mac or PC, in which case their styles will carry across.

Combining text and images

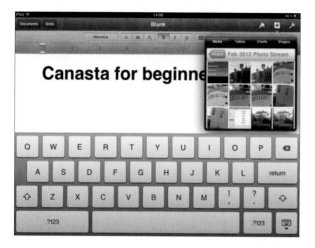

1. Pages is more than a dumb word processor: it shares many features with its desktop counterpart, bringing low-level page design to the iPad. Here we're going to create a document heading by combining text and a photo. The text is already in place, so we just need to select our photo by tapping the image icon and selecting from our library.

2. Now we need to re-size the image to fit our layout. Do this by tapping it once to bring up the drag handles (blue dots on the corners and edges) and dragging them to the appropriate position. Notice how the image dimensions are detailed beside the handle, and how dotted guide lines keep our dragging finger on course.

3. Our layout looked a bit flat, so we have added a text box, again from the image icon menu, and typed our headline into the space. We changed the colour to yellow so that it showed up better on the background. By default floating text boxes have a black border, which looks out of place on our image, so with the box still selected we've tapped the 'i' icon and selected the first option – no frame.

4. Our styling is complete. To finish it off nicely we have right-aligned the text and inserted a carriage return after the word Canasta so that the words fit within the space of the green table cloth. When we deselect the box, only the text will remain visible. It remains editable at all times, though, and can be repositioned anywhere within the document should you change your mind later.

Editing Pages templates

1. Pages ships with a choice of 16 templates (including the plain empty page we used for our Canasta file) that you can use as jumping-off points for more complex documents by swapping out existing elements. Here we're using the Modern Photo Letter template. We've tapped the icon on the photo so that we can pick a replacement from our library.

2. As well as placeholder images, there is plenty of placeholder text on each template. Tapping on any one of these highlight the complete block, however many lines it covers, so that you can type directly onto the page and it will be swapped out. Alternatively, if you've previously copied some text tap *Paste* to drop it in its place.

3. Although the layouts look pretty fixed, you can change the size and position of boxes and image frames, and move the indents, tabs and margins. Indents, tabs and margins are set on the ruler; drag the pointers along the scale to move them. Each will only affect the active line or paragraph, so if you need to re-align several blocks, select them all before moving the ruler markers.

When you've added several pages to a document, you can move more quickly from one page to another by holding your thumb in the margin and dragging up and down, rather than by swiping up and down the page with a finger. This calls up a spyglass that shows thumbnails of each page in your document. When you reach the one you want to work on, release your thumb from the screen.

Accessing files on a WebDAV server

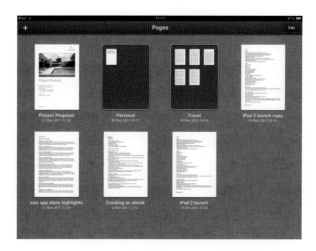

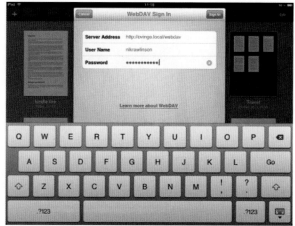

1. Pages has a simple yet accomplished file management system perfectly tuned to navigation with a fingertip. Since the arrival of iCloud it also automatically backs up your documents to an off-site server. However, business users will find it more convenient to organise their documents on their own WebDAV server. Here, we'll show you how.

2. Our WebDAV server is hosted locally on a corporate server, in this case running Mac OS X Lion Server. The precise address of your server will depend on your own company's settings, but to connect tap the '+' button on the toolbar and select *Copy from WebDAV*, then enter your server's address, plus your username and password, then tap *Sign In*.

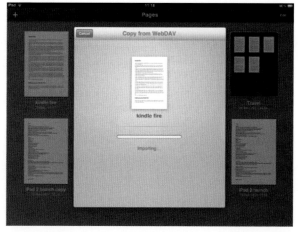

3. Pages will verify your credentials and connect to the server, presenting you with a familiar file and folder structure. Tap through the folders until you find the document you want to use. You may well find that you are presented with more top level folders than expected, as some WebDAV servers – ours included – will give you access to your home folder, as well as any shared document folders.

4. Having found the file you want to use, tap it once to copy it from the server to your iPad. You can't work directly on the file where it's stored on the server as this may cause conflicts with other users who could try to access it at the same time. When the download has completed, your personal copy of the document will be stored in the regular Pages file structure ready for you to start work.

Copying completed work back to the server

Because you can't work on files in situ, you need to copy them to your iPad before they're made available. When you've finished working on them, therefore, you have several options of what to do next.

If you've signed up for a free iCloud account then your document will be automatically uploaded to Apple's servers as soon as you return to the file management screen, and you're still free to email it to a colleague or copy it to a format that would allow you to download it from your tablet using the Files and Documents Sharing pane in iTunes on your computer.

However, as we originally copied our file from a WebDAV server it makes more sense for us to upload the amended version back to the server, both so that it's ready for us to access again in the future on the iPad or any other service capable of logging in to an account on the server, and so that it can be shared with other users.

Fortunately Pages already knows our login credentials from when we downloaded the file in the first place, so we can get started right away.

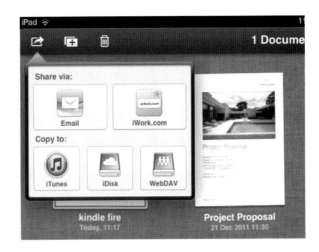

1. Start by tapping the *Edit* button on the far right of the Pages file manager screen, and then select the document you have just finished working on. It will be highlighted with a yellow border. Now tap the share button (the rectangle with a curved arrow curling out of it) and select *WebDAV* from the *Copy to:* section.

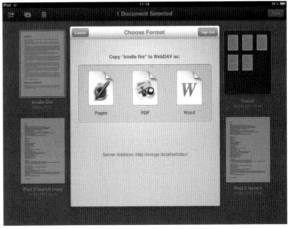

2. Assuming you're still logged in to your account you'll be able to navigate through the same folders as you did when finding your file in the first place. Note that you can only log in to one WebDAV server at a time, so if you want to copy your edited document to a new location you'll need to tap *Sign out* and provide your credentials for that other location.

3. When you have found the folder in which you want to save the file, tap the *Copy* button on the dialogue's heading bar and then select the format in which you want to save it. Although Pages has its own native format, Windows users won't be able to access this as there's no PC version of iWork. Select Word if you're happy for them to edit your file, or PDF if maintaining your exact layout is most important.

Numbers

Numbers is a sophisticated spreadsheet with great graphing tools to help you get a grip on your financial situation. It also has four rather clever keyboards that greatly ease the task of entering data.

I f you've used Numbers on the Mac, you'll know what a revolutionary piece of software it is. It completely rethinks the way that spreadsheets work, giving you access to several tables on a single sheet, rather than just several sheets in a single document, each with only one table.

Numbers ships with 16 different templates that take a lot of the hard work out of starting a new spreadsheet. Together they cover every base, with pre-designed sheets for organising teams, invoicing and submitting expense reports, among others.

The most useful remains the blank table that presents you with an empty page. Crucially, this doesn't occupy the whole sheet in your document, but only a portion of it. Tapping it calls up handles at the bottom and right-hand edge, which when dragged enlarge or reduce the size of the table on the sheet. Tabs across the top of the screen let you add new sheets to the document, each of which can contain several other tables.

To enter data you start by double-tapping on a cell. This calls up the familiar entry bar that you'll know from Excel or Numbers on regular desktop computers. Crucially, though, you'll find it supplemented by four buttons to the left. These are for entering numbers, time and date, text, and equations (*see facing page*).

Tapping through them, you'll see that each one changes the keyboard that appears below the entry box. If spreadsheets aren't your strong point, there's plenty of help to be had through each one. Open the equations entry field, for example, and tap on Functions to call up a

list of the commands that Numbers understands, from the fairly simple *SUM*, used to add, multiply, subtract and so on, to more complex *IF* functions that test conditions within cells in your spreadsheet and act upon its findings.

As with Pages and Keynote, you can incorporate other media into your documents, including photos, shapes and graphs drawn up using the data in tables on your various spreadsheet pages. Graphs are easily tailored by dragging your finger across the cells in your tables to set the range to be displayed within them, while cycling through the various pages in the Charts panel of the media drop-down box lets you choose the colour scheme used to illustrate each one (*above right*).

Cells can be formatted en masse or individually by tapping or drag-selecting and then tapping the '*i*' button on the toolbar. This opens up a menu from which you can choose common data types, such as numbers, currency, percentages and so on. More interestingly, though, you can also insert check boxes into cells in your spreadsheet that can be ticked and unticked using the digits 1 and 0, and star ratings of the kind you find on the iTunes Store that are awarded using the numbers 0 to 5.

Like Pages and Keynote, Numbers has export options for sharing your work with other applications. Available export formats include Numbers, which will only be of use to anyone with Numbers on a Mac, alongside Excel .xls for Mac and PCs and the almost universal PDF format. It also synchronies via iCloud so that any spreadsheets you create or edit on your iPad also appear on your iPhone or iPod touch.

Above: Numbers isn't all about digits and decimal points. Its sophisticated graphing tools help you illustrate what your workings mean in a more engaging and immediately understandable fashion. There's a wide range of graph types to choose from, with one for every situation.

Below: With four specialised keyboards that you can switch between at will, Numbers greatly eases the task of entering almost any kind of data. These keyboards are one of the features that make this perhaps the most versatile spreadsheet available on the iPad.

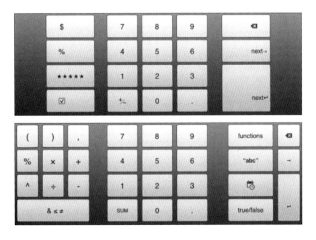

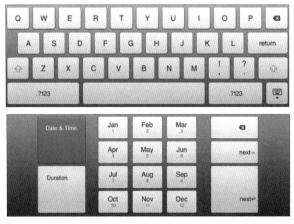

Working in Numbers

When Apple came up with the idea for Numbers it completely re-thought the way spreadsheets should work. The program is a masterstroke of design that transfers very successfully to the iPad, as we'll show you here.

Understanding the Numbers interface

Spreadsheets
Tap to return to file manager and create new documents.

Sheets
Tap to switch between sheets; tap the '+' tab to create new ones.

Styles
Access pre-set styles, or tweak the current formatting.

Media
Insert shapes, tables and charts. Access your photo library.

Tools
Change document settings and margins, output to a shared printer and more.

iPad			08:39		99%
Spreadsheets	Undo		Travel Planner		
Activity List		Reservations	Packing List	+	

Hawaiian Vacation 2012
Activity List

Activities

Date	Time	Activity	Location	Contact	Notes
12/16/12	2:00 PM	Magic Sands Beach	Kona Coast	Public	Beach with surfing, sailing, shops &

Numbers fundamentals

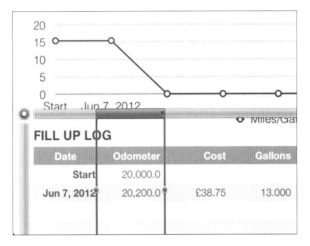

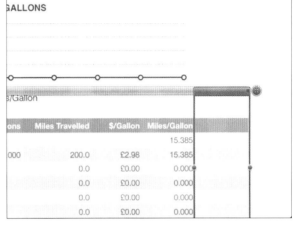

1. It's not immediately obvious how you change the size of a column or row in Numbers. Tap the active table, though, and up pops a set of bars above and to the left. Tap this above the column, or to the left of the cell you want to resize, to select the column or row, and then use the drag handle on the right or bottom to enlarge or shrink it.

2. A similar principle applies to increasing the size of your active table. With the bars visible you'll see a spot appear to the right of the columns and below the rows. Tapping this, or dragging it down or to the right, adds a new row and column respectively. You can extend the table beyond the edge of the screen and scroll to access the new cells.

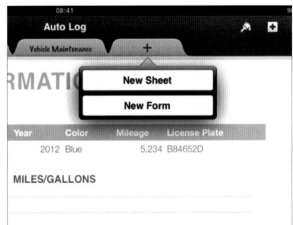

3. To make further changes, use the menu that pops up above the column or the first cell of a row. This lets you copy and paste complete rows and columns, insert new ones or delete the selected group of cells. To quickly adjust the width of a column or the height of a row so that it fits its contents, tap *Fit*. If you have any wrapped text within the column, the wrap point will be used to determine the width.

4. Unlike Excel and other conventional spreadsheets, Numbers lets you put several discrete tables on each sheet within your document. You can add new sheets to your document to help organise your various tables by tapping the '+' on the final tab to the right of the bar that runs across the top of your active page. *New Form*, the other option, is used for data collection.

Creating a savings plan in Numbers for iPad

1. Numbers comes packed with a series of templates, one of which is a useful Personal Savings spreadsheet. However, this can be a little more complex for some, so we're going to create our own and, in the process, learn how to use many of Numbers' key formatting features. For now, then, tap *Blank* to open a new empty spreadsheet.

2. Here we've resized the first table on our opening sheet by dragging the column spot to the left. We have also entered some headings in the first column and given the table a title: *Savings plan*. By default this would wrap within the column as we've set it in 36pt text. To solve this, we've opened the formatting panel and set *Wrap Text in Cell* to *OFF*.

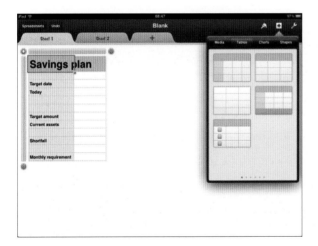

3. That first table is going to hold a summary of the rest of our spreadsheet, drawing data from other tables. We still need to create those other tables, so tap on the toolbar's media button and select the *Tables* tab. We want a table with header cells on both the rows and columns. That's the first option, so we'll tap the table at the top of the left-hand column here.

4. By default, our table is given a header – in this case Table 2, although we can change it to something more appropriate if we want to. However, as we want all of the tables in our spreadsheet to match we'll get rid of this and instead type the header in the top row of cells. Tap once on the table to select it and then tap the 'i' button, followed by *Table | Table Options* and turn off *Table Name*.

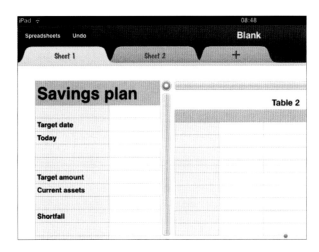

5. Numbers dropped our table in a random location, so we need to align it with the existing *Savings plan* table. We do this by simply dragging it using the spot in the top left corner. When it's lined up with other elements on the sheet it's overlaid by yellow guidelines. Here the lines are indicating that the vertical centres of each table are aligned.

6. With each of our tables in place we can now start entering our data. We'll begin with the liabilities. Notice how we have selected the £ data type on the left of the keyboard to enter financial figures. There are two *next* buttons on the right. The first moves horizontally; the second, vertically. We'll use the second to move down our column as we enter data.

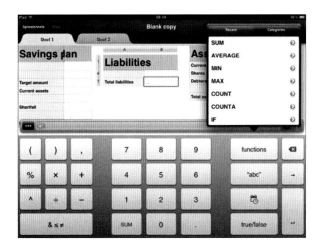

7. Having entered all of our liabilities we can now add them up so that we can use the total in our summary table. We therefore tap in the cell beside *Total liabilities* and tap the '-' button at the left of the formula entry bar so that we can type in an equation. To save us time, Numbers is pre-populated with several ready-formed formulae, so we'll tap the *functions* button and select *SUM*.

8. Numbers drops the SUM formula opener into the formula bar, along with a placeholder for the variables that will comprise our equation. To swap them out for our the cells containing our liabilities, we tap in the cell containing the first – the outstanding mortgage value – and then drag down the spot in the bottom right corner to encompass all of our values.

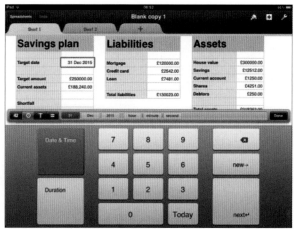

9. Over the next few steps we're going to work with a lot of different data types, but we'll start by performing a sum on data drawn from two different tables by tapping in the cell beside *Current assets* on the *Savings plan* table and subtracting our *Total liabilities* from our *Total assets* by drawing in data from their respective tables.

10. Now we're going to set ourself some targets. We'll start by tapping in the *Target date* variable cell and then tap the clock on the formula bar to call up the time and date keyboard. We now just step through the various boxes on the formula bar, tapping the date, month and year and using the context-sensitive keyboard. We can ignore hour, minute and second.

11. Now we need a few extra cells so that we can do some calculations to work out how long we still have in which to reach our savings goal. To do this we tap in the row below the target date entry and then tap the portion of the bar to its left. From this we tap *Insert* to add a new row. We'll repeat this operation another two times to add two blank rows to the spreadsheet.

12. We've added the current date to one of those new cells by using the time and date keyboard's dedicated *TODAY* button, which draws its data from the iPad's internal clock. Although we are now working with dates rather than regular numbers we can still do some maths on them. We need to know how much time we have left on our side, so subtract today from the target date.

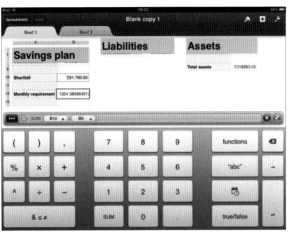

13. The result is 1402 days, which is a very comfortable margin. However, in a world where most of us are paid a monthly rather than daily wage it's not all that meaningful. We'll therefore manually tweak that sum by bracketing the B3 and B4 variables and dividing the result by 30. Not all months consist of 30 days, but it gives us a fair idea of what we need to save.

14. With a shortfall of £61,760 from our savings target, and 47 months in which to achieve our goal, Numbers helpfully tells us that we need to save 1321.540656205... currency units. This isn't quite the answer we are looking for, as the number is far too long to be of any use as we only have 100 units in each pound.

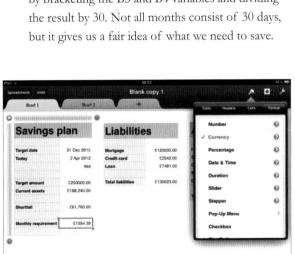

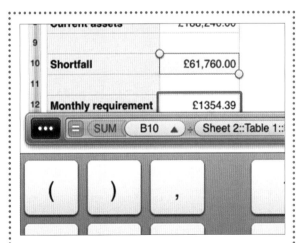

15. We could reduce the number of decimal places in our result, but there's a better, more convenient way to do it that also solves the problem of the missing currency denominator. So, to kill those two birds with a single digital stone, we'll make sure the result is selected and then tap the '*i*' button, followed by *Format*. Now we just need pick *Currency* from the list of options.

In this workthrough we have copied data between tables, but you can use the same principle to also draw data from other pages within the spreadsheet entirely. Do this by tapping in the destination cell that will contain the result of your sum, start your sum and switch to the sheet from which you want to draw your data. Tap on the relevant cell, and when you've finished hit next to go back to your sum.

Keynote

Anyone who has to present for a living understands the importance of a good set of slides. With Keynote you can build your own on the move, even if your Mac or PC has been safely left back at the office.

Keynote is Apple's presentation tool – its version of Microsoft's own PowerPoint. Unlike the other iPad iWork applications it only works one way around: landscape. That's because its content – the slides that you create – are designed to be shown on a regular computer monitor.

Well aware that not everybody is a skilled designer, Apple has included 12 high quality templates with the application. This is fewer than you'll find in the regular Mac-based version of Keynote, but if you're familiar with the desktop / laptop edition you will find that a number of familiar favourites have nonetheless made the transition to this mobile variant, including Chalkboard, Modern Portfolio and Showroom.

When you're building your presentation, the interface is split into two, with a channel for organising your slides on the left, and a larger area for the actual design of your slides to the right.

Apple has thought very carefully about the way that you would create slides without the use of a mouse, and has made everything easy to drive with the finger. A '+' button at the bottom of the organiser channel lets you add new slides, and tapping it will bring up a list of the different slide variations in your theme. Tap the one you want and it appears in the organiser channel.

Editing the slides themselves is just as easy. Tapping in a text area calls up the keyboard, allowing you to type directly onto the slide with full access to formatting and bullets. You can also change the way that your text appears on the screen for greater impact.

Again many of the familiar options from Keynote's Mac edition are present here, including Blast, Appear and Compress. You can tweak the speed at which the build completes and whether it happens manually ('On Tap') or automatically ('After Transition') in each instance.

Photos – for what is a presentation without images? – are pulled in from your Photo Albums and can be resized on the slide itself. You can zoom in to a precise level and then pull the edges of the constraining frame towards the centre or edges of your slide so that the image is properly cropped. You can also apply effects such as concave and convex curls and drop shadows.

The iPad screen is an excellent medium on which to showcase your presentation, and if you buy the optional VGA or HDMI connection kit you can hook it up to a regular monitor or a projector for showing to larger groups. You can also use iOS 5's built-in AirPlay feature to send the output to an Apple TV-equipped television set. If you would rather show it on your Mac or a PC you can export it – as you can with the files created in Pages and Numbers. Sadly for PC users, you can't export your work as a PowerPoint .ppt or .pptx file, but only in Keynote or PDF format, which really means that if you don't have a Mac with Keynote you must use PDF.

The iPad version of Keynote is among the most versatile and accomplished slide-design tools we have seen on any platform – not just on a mobile device. Its integration with Apple's free iCloud service now also means that any document you create on your iPad will be automatically synchronised to an iPhone or iPod touch.

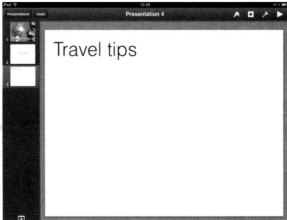

8.   We don't need to do anything more to our second slide as it's designed to be a title card for the new section. However, we do want to define a transition between this and the one that follows. We want to keep the 'Travel tips' header so that it appears on every slide in the section, so we'll use a special kind of transition called Magic Move. This first duplicates your existing slide and then keeps track of the items it contains as you move them to new positions on the copy. You can delete any elements that you don't want – in our case 'for first-time visitors' – and they'll disappear during the transition. We have therefore moved the Travel tips header up towards the top of the slide where it will form the basis of the slides that follow.

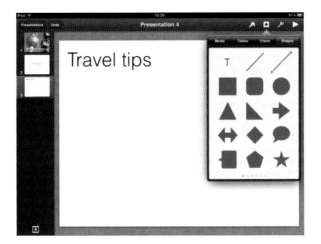

9.   We need to add some more text to the page. As there's no mouse pointer on the iPad you can't simply click on the slide and start typing. Instead, you need to draw out a text box to hold your new content, drag it into position and then fill with whatever words you want to use. Text boxes are considered regular shapes, so are found by tapping the media button, followed by *Shapes* and the 'T'.

10.   We've entered our text as a series of bullet points. Breaking up your information in this way helps your audience to assimilate it more effectively as they're not presented with a daunting block of solid text. Even so, being presented with three points at once can be overwhelming, so we'll introduce them gradually with a 'build in' by selecting the text frame and tapping the transition diamonds again.

11. We've chosen to have each bullet point fade into view by selecting the dissolve effect. Now we need to choose on the *Options* pane how long each dissolve should last (1 second) and what should trigger them. We want them to appear each time we tap the screen. Choosing *After Transition* would cause them to fade in one after another.

12. Finally, how should they be grouped during the transition? The default is *All at Once*, which would fade in the complete text box. We want them one bullet point at a time so that we can talk our audience through each one before the next is displayed. We have therefore tapped the *Delivery* tab and selected *By Bullet*.

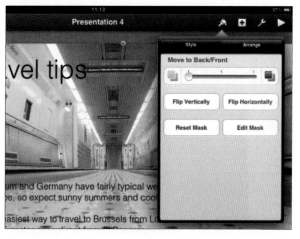

13. Our black bullets on a white background are easy to read, but not very engaging. As we're encouraging people to use trains we'll underlay the whole slide with a picture of the inside of a Channel Tunnel Shuttle. We've imported one of these into our iPad photo library and used the Gallery button on the toolbar to add it to our slide. However, this introduces a problem: it's on top of the text.

14. Fortunately Keynote has this covered. With the image still selected, and now scaled to fill the whole slide, tapping the '*i*' button calls up its settings. We can ignore the *Style* pane unless we want to set a border and instead simply tap *Arrange*. Here, dragging the slider at the top of the pane will send the image to the bottom of the object stack, beneath everything else on the slide.

15. Now we just need to tell Keynote how it should handle the image's appearance. At the moment it will only appear at the very last moment, after the Magic Move transition and the dissolve of our bullet points, as it was the last thing we added. We can fix this by selecting the image and tapping the transition diamonds. We've selected dissolve as our transition type on the *Effects* tab so that it fades into view rather than popping up. We've set the transition to complete over the course of 1 second, firing automatically as soon as the previous transition completes (*above left*). However, at the moment the previous transition is still the final bullet. Tapping on Order therefore lets us drag the Image to the top of the list so that it dissolves into view before the bullets, in time with the Magic Move (*above right*).

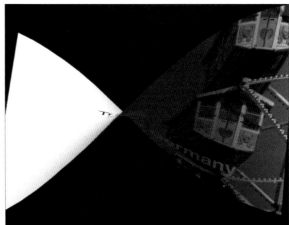

16. If you're going to be presenting your slides on a larger screen connected by means of a video adapter, or a projector, take advantage of the presenter notes feature to tap out some aides memoire for yourself. These will be displayed on your iPad screen, along with controls for moving backwards and forwards through the presentation, while the slides themselves will be sent to the output device.

17. All of the elements are now in place for us to carry on building slides until we reach the end of our presentation. With everything written and checked, it's time to unleash it on our audience. Tapping the play icon gives over the whole of your screen to your slides, which switch out one for the next with the transitions you chose (above, the twist transition in action). Have confidence, and knock 'em dead!

Edit video in iMovie

Apple's video editing tool, iMovie, first appeared on the iMac. Now, though, it's also available on the iPhone and iPad, allowing you to edit videos shot on either device directly, and then share them with friends and family over the web.

Understanding the iMovie interface

Clip bin
Compatible video on your iPad appears here for editing.

Media
Switch between video, still photos and music as you build your movie.

Monitor
Play back your movie in real time during the editing process.

Transition
The point at which one clip fades into the next.

Timeline
Here's where you arrange your clips to build your video.

Settings
Change the movie style and your fade-in and -out settings in here.

Importing video into iMovie

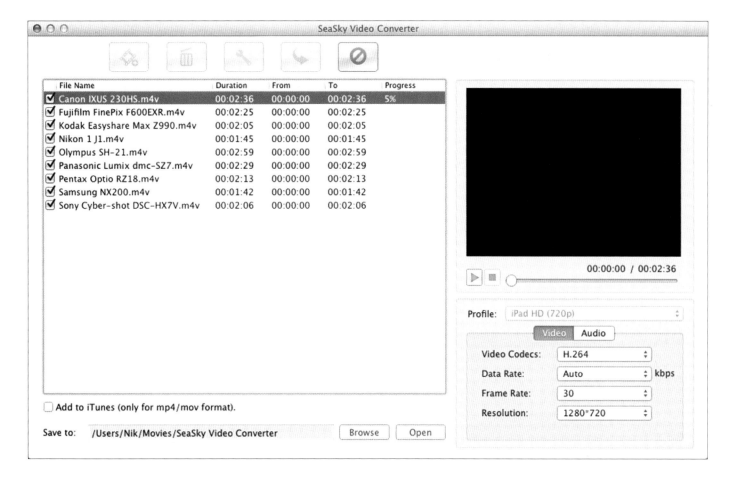

iMovie on the iPad is designed for editing movies shot using the iPad's integrated cameras. This isn't as convenient as it is on the iPhone, as the iPad is too bulky to be manipulated easily in the quest to capture the footage for your cinematic masterpiece.

It's therefore often easier to shoot your video files on a separate camera – even a consumer stills camera will often be up to the job of shooting suitable footage – and importing it to your iPad for later editing.

Unfortunately, the iPad is quite picky about the video formats it will work with, and iMovie is even more selective. In all likelihood, then, you'll need to first convert your assets before you can use them in iMovie.

Footage shot on an iPhone naturally transfers well and works without a glitch in iMovie. However, anything shot with an external device will likely need some work before it's sent to your iPad. There are video conversion utilities for both Windows and the Mac that can do this.

Here we're using SeaSky Video Converter on the Mac, which is available in trial format if you don't want to buy it outright immediately. We have stacked up all of the clips that we want to use in the input bin on the left of the interface and chosen our output settings on the right. Ideally you need your footage to be output as a Quicktime compatible .mov-format video.

Once the conversion is complete, you'll need to transfer the footage to your iPad. This is done either by dragging it into iPhoto and synchronising your iPad through iTunes, which copies all videos in selected iPhoto albums to your device, or by opting for manual management of movies and music through the iTunes interface and then dragging your footage across to the iPad in the iTunes sidebar.

It goes without saying that you should only ever work with footage for which you own the rights in any video editing application, to avoid infringing owners' copyright.

Editing your first movie

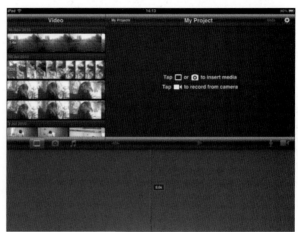

1. iMovie is an app with a great sense of style. This is the project organisation screen. Each of your edited movies is presented as a poster on a cinema wall. At the moment we don't have any movies in place, so tap the '+' button, either in the grey box or at the bottom of the screen, to start work on editing a new video.

2. Here's iMovie's opening editing view. All of the footage available to us is organised in the clip bin on the top left of the screen. The large window to the right is the preview monitor, where we'll see our movie come together, while the large area at the bottom is the timeline where we arrange the clips. The red line represents the playhead.

3. Here we're previewing a clip so we can be sure it's the one we want to use. We're doing this by holding down our finger on the footage in the clip bin and dragging our finger left and right across it to scrub the video stream. The point at which our finger sits at any time is displayed in the preview monitor.

4. Now that we know we've found the clip we want to use we only need tap once to import it into our movie. Tapping again on the blue arrow drops it onto the timeline. If we only want to import a portion of the clip, we first drag in the yellow dots (in the top left and bottom right corner of the clip selection) towards the centre to trim the start and end, called the 'in' and 'out' points.

5. With our first clip in place we need to have a think about how we want our overall project to look. Tapping the cog button on the iMovie toolbar calls up the Project Settings. Here we can select the theme that we want to use by sliding past the various options in the top section of the dialogue and choose various options using the slide switches below. We have chosen the Travel theme, which encompasses set transitions, text styles and associated music. We've turned on fade in and out from black to bookend the finished video.

6. We've now got to the point where we're working with the second scene of our movie. Again we previewed it in the clip bin, selected the portion we wanted to use, and then tapped to add it to the timeline. It's automatically positioned after our first clip. The icon you can see between the two clips represents the transition. By default this uses the standard transition associated with our chosen theme – Travel – but, as we'll see over the page, we can tailor this to a high degree, changing both the speed and the style to meet our needs.

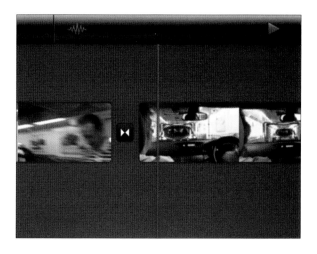

7. Tapping the transition icon and then tapping the double-headed arrow that appears lets us tweak the point where the transition begins and ends on our two merged clips (*above*). The top spot marks the point where our first clip fades out; dragging it left sets it earlier into the first clip. The bottom spot marks the point where the second clip fades in; dragging it right sets it later into the second clip.

8. Once we've perfected our in and out points we can tap the double-ended arrow again to merge the clips together so that our selected in- and out-points line up with one another. Double-tapping the icon quickly then calls up the transition settings, allowing us to choose how quickly the fade from the first clip to the next should complete, or choose a different transition style altogether.

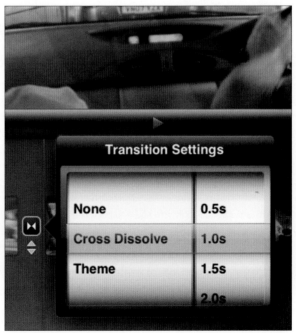

9. You're not restricted to only using video. iMovie can also work with still photos drawn from your camera roll or Photo Stream. Tap the camera icon below the clip bin to switch to photos, and then tap each image in turn to add it to the timeline. Tapping a photo on the timeline calls up grab spots that you can use to lengthen or shorten its duration in the movie.

10. To keep things interesting, iMovie automatically pans and zooms your images across the screen, rather than leaving them static. To control the direction and amount of zoom, tap the *Start* and *End* buttons on the image itself in the preview monitor and then pinch, unpinch and drag to change the default positions.

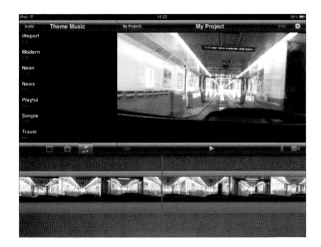
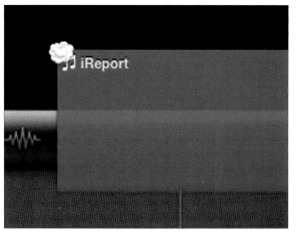

11. Our movie is coming along nicely now. We have our footage in place, and can shoot anything that we don't yet have from within iMovie itself by tapping the video camera icon on the far right-hand end of the toolbar just below the preview monitor. What we're lacking, though, is a dynamic soundtrack that will tie everything together; at the moment our movie just jumps from one clip to the next, taking their raw soundtracks with them. Tapping the musical note icon below the clip bin switches to the audio library from which we can select tracks from our iPad music collection, or the sound effects and theme music that shipped as part of iMovie. Double-tap a track to add it to your movie, at which point the parts of the movie that it applies to will adopt a fat green border (*above left*). To remove a track or sound effect, drag it away from the timeline (*above right*).

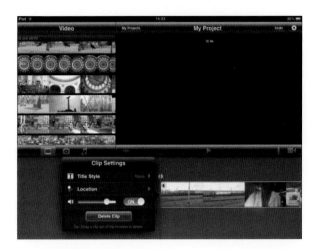

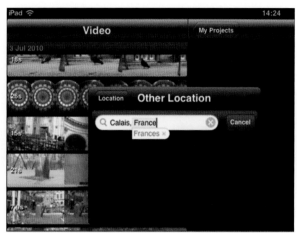

12. We're almost there. Our clips have been assembled, our photos are in place and we've chosen an underlying soundtrack for our movie. Adding some extra data, though, allows us to apply text to our images and video sections, just like they do on TV. The first step is to double-tap one of our clips to call up its settings.

13. Tapping *Location* lets us enter a place name. Here we're changing the settings for the opening shot of our video, which shows a Shuttle train coming out of the Channel Tunnel at Calais, so we have searched for Calais, France. iMovie wants to autocorrect this to Frances, so we'll tap the correct popup to dismiss it.

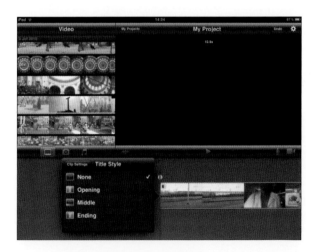

14. Stepping back to the settings dialogue, we'll now add a title by tapping *Title Style*. Each style is different, and the exact finished appearance will depend on which movie theme you chose in step 5, as they are designed to complement your chosen subject. We want to create the opening titles of our film, so we'll tap *Opening...*

15. ...and here's the graphic we'll be working with. Our moving video has been dropped into a postcard surround, it's pinpointed France on the map from the data we entered in step 13, and we're adding our title – *A Trip To Europe* – in the space at the bottom of the title card. When we play back our video it will zoom in on the footage in the postcard at the end of the opening clip.

16. We can add titles at any point in our movie. This would be useful if we were to interview anyone and wanted to put their name at the bottom of the screen, as is common practice on news programmes and documentaries. In this case, though, we just want to help people understand what the locations in our video represent and where our photos were taken. Here we have tapped on a still photo and chosen the *Middle* title style. This overlays the bottom quarter of the picture with another travel-styled graphic onto which we've been able to type the name of the place in the photo. This is the last step in creating our movie.

17. With all of our titles in place we can now sit back and preview the results of our work. Tap the *My Projects* button above the preview monitor to go back to the opening iMovie screen and select the cinema poster that represents the movie you've just created. Tap the play button to watch it full screen and make sure you're happy with what you've created. If not, you can still go back and tweak it.

18. When you're satisfied with your creation, it's time to show off to your friends and family. Tapping the share button, which looks like a curved arrow coming out of a box, you can directly upload your video to your account on YouTube or Vimeo, send it to CNN if it's a newsworthy event, or add it to your Facebook timeline. Alternatively, to keep it private, save it to your Camera Roll or export it to iTunes.

Edit pictures in iPhoto

Apple introduced the tablet-centric iPhoto alongside the new iPad, but it also works on the iPad 2, allowing you to perform accomplished editing tasks by tapping and swiping, without even loading your pictures on your Mac or PC.

Understanding the iPhoto interface

Thumbnails
Select an image to edit from this strip of photos stored locally

Edit window
Here's where you'll do most of your work, applying your changes

Tools
Dynamic area that lets you select tools related to your current task

Share
Send your edited image to your choice of photo sharing services

Show original
Switch between your edits and original to review your changes

Edit
Open the loaded image in a format that allows it to be edited

Editing pictures with iPhoto

1. iPhoto works with pictures already on your iPad, which are organised into albums on a series of glass shelves. Tap an album to view its contents to get yourself started, and then choose which picture you want to work with.

2. The downward arrow above the strip of images lets you choose which ones are displayed. We've selected All Photos. Having chosen the picture we want to edit, though, we'll now tap the toolbar's blue grid icon to hide the thumbnails.

3. If you need a closer look at any part of your image, tapping the screen with two fingers simultaneously calls up the magnifier. Rotating this changes the magnification up to 3x. Tap anywhere else on the screen to dismiss it.

4. One of the easiest ways to get images onto your iPad is to transfer them using Photo Stream. Dropping them into a linked folder on your PC, or into iPhoto or Aperture on your Mac, copies them to your iPad, allowing you to use a wider choice of cameras. Tapping '*i*' reveals the camera, shooting conditions, and other information about the image.

5. And if you need any more information about the iPhoto interface while you're working on your pictures, tap the '*?*' to call up pointers. Tapping the circles at the end of each help point reveals more extensive help. Once you're comfortable with the interface, tap the *Edit* button at the end of the toolbar to start work.

6. The most effective change you can make is often Auto Enhance, which seeks to balance the colours and levels in the image to produce a punchy, more satisfying result. Tap the magic wand in the central group of controls on the bottom toolbar to select Auto Enhance. When it's finished, tapping the curled page icon beside the *Edit* button lets you compare the result with your original.

7. If you're happy with the result then it makes sense to apply it to other pictures taken under the same conditions as they'll share many common lighting and colour characteristics. Tap the cog icon and select *Copy Exposure, Color and Effect*, and then switch to the image to which you'd like to apply the exact same settings, tap the cog again and this time select *Paste Exposure, Color and Effect*.

8. Although Auto Enhance is very effective, there are many times when you'll want to make manual adjustments to your image. Tap the paint palette icon to open the colour controls. This is where iPhoto starts to get really clever. Either drag the individual sliders for saturation, blue skies, greens or skin tones, or place your finger on a portion of your image to have iPhoto detect the underlying content. You can then drag left, right, up or down to change the colour setting relevant to just that part of the image.

9. So far, all of our changes have been applied across the whole canvas, so they apply to every part of the image equally. Often, though, we'll only want to edit a small portion of the image. This is where the iPhoto brushes come in to play, as they let you selectively brush changes onto specific parts of the picture. Tap the toolbar's brushes icon to call them up and select the adjustment you want to make. In our case, we'll use the 'Sharpen' brush to sharpen up the nose, whiskers and eyes of this cat image, as that's where you naturally look first.

10. Get busy painting on your changes, but it might not be immediately obvious what effect your brushed changes are having, so to make it easier to see where you've already been working, tap the cog icon to open the brush settings and switch on Brush Strokes, which overlays the image with a red dye. While here you can also change the degree to which the change is applied, and cut time by applying it across the whole image.

11. Finally we're going to straighten and crop our image. We start by tapping the crop icon, which is the crossed set squares on the far left of the toolbar, which calls up a grid overlay. Dragging the corners or edges of this in or out shrinks and enlarges the portion of the image that is to be retained after the crop. Notice also the wheel at the bottom of the image. Turning this rotates the image so that we can straighten it up, although you can also tap it once and then tilt your iPad to achieve the same thing.

12. We're pretty pleased with our results, so it's only right that we should share them with our friends. Fortunately iPhoto has several sharing options built in, which take advantage of popular photo sharing sites, email and a new beam feature that sends them directly to other iPhoto users. For the moment we're going to use Flickr.

13. We need to select which photos to send to our account by tapping the ones we want in the thumbnail browser. We only want to send the one we've just finished editing, so we don't need to tap the *Range* button. Instead we'll just tap the thumbnail with the toolbox on it and move on to the next step.

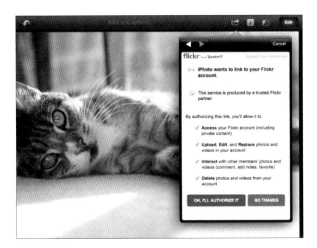

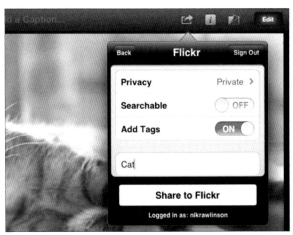

14. As this is the first time we'll be uploading a picture from iPhoto to our Flickr account we need to authorise access to our Photo Stream. Having entered our Yahoo login details (you'll need a Yahoo account) it shows the Flickr authorisation dialogue, allowing us to choose whether or not iPhoto can perform actions on our account.

15. We've authorised it, so now we need to decide how the image should be filed. We want to keep it private and out of Flickr's search engine, but we also want to tag it so that we can find it ourselves later. We've therefore tapped the *Add Tags* slider and are using the box below to label it. When we're done we'll tap the *Share to Flickr* button.

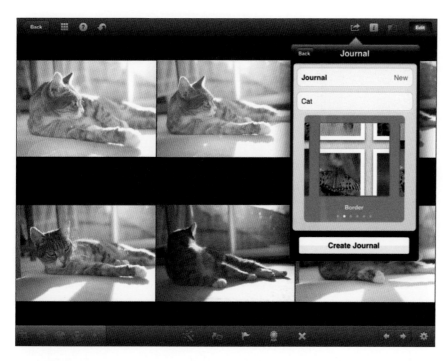

16. iPhoto also introduces a new sharing tool: Journals. These even have their own dedicated screen on the glass-shelved file management screen. Again they're selected from the share button on the toolbar, and they come in a variety of styles. You can choose which style to apply to your Journal by swiping through them in the window. When you've found one you like, and you've named the Journal, tap *Create Journal*.

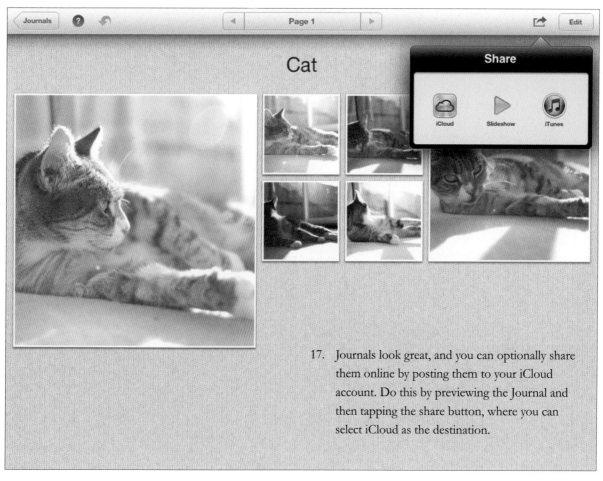

17. Journals look great, and you can optionally share them online by posting them to your iCloud account. Do this by previewing the Journal and then tapping the share button, where you can select iCloud as the destination.

iPhoto tools in more detail

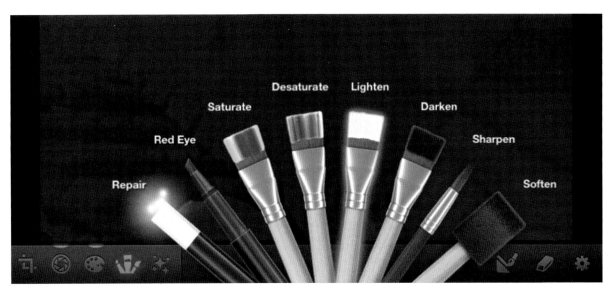

Correction tools (*above*) are used either to make a poorly-shot picture more closely resemble the original subject, or balance certain aspects of a dull or incorrectly-exposed photo. Red eye reduces the effect of flash on eyes; saturate and desaturate change the strength of colours, lighten and darken adjust the overall tone, and sharpen and soften highlight or blur fine detail. Each can be brushed on individually and with varying degrees of strength.

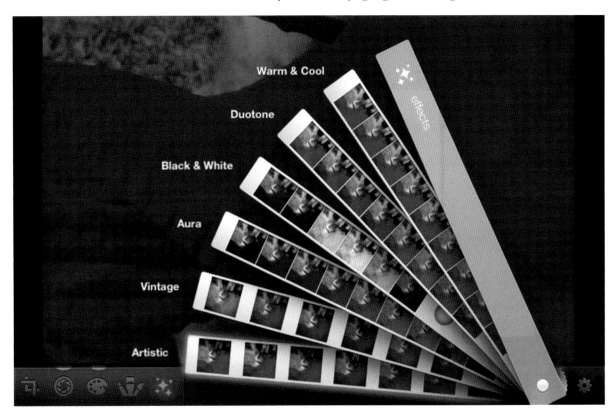

Effects (*above*) apply more far-reaching and radical adjustments to the picture. They are applied on a canvas-wide basis so that they can balance out each of the adjusted tones across your whole shot. After selecting one of the sample swatches, sliding your finger across the thumbnail previews the type and strength of the applied effect.

Composing in GarageBand

GarageBand's sophisticated tools and pre-recorded loops make it easy to lay down impressive, professional-sounding tracks using nothing more than an iPad, a finger and some very inexpensive software.

Understanding the GarageBand interface

Tracks
Thumbnails representing each track in your song

Recordings
Waveforms of the loops and recordings in your composition

Mode
Switch between loop and recording modes for composition

Volume
Graphical mirror of the iPad's hardware volume rocker switch

Loops
Open the loops library to select assets for use in your song

Settings
Change attributes and settings of the currently-selected track

How to record a track in GarageBand

1. If you've used any iLife or iWork app then much of GarageBand's way of working will be familiar to you already. It uses Apple's system of taps and swipes to create, delete and arrange files. The starting point is your library of songs. To add a new one, tap the '+' icon and select *New Song* from the drop-down menu.

2. We're going to create our song using Apple's pre-defined loops, but we still need to select an instrument to get started. This will create the first track in our song. It doesn't really matter which we choose at this point, so we'll scroll through them to have a look at what's available for future reference.

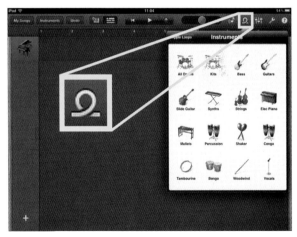

3. We've selected the Smart Keyboard shown in step 2. This is its interface. You can play with its features to help yourself get used to the way that GarageBand works, but avoid tapping the toolbar's record button just yet, as you don't want to start laying down a track at this stage. When you're comfortable with the interface, switch to the tracks layout by tapping the button we've circled above.

4. This is the track view where all of the instruments we have recorded using GarageBand will send their output. For those with little or no musical talent it's also the place to turn if you want to drag and drop pre-recorded loops onto the stave to build up a track using Apple's bundled material. Tap the loops button indicated above to call up the available instruments and select *Synths* to get started.

5. You can audition each loop for every instrument in the library by tapping it in the lower portion of the Loops dialogue. Tap through them until you find one that you like the sound of. The bars measurement to the right of each name tells you how long each one lasts. To use a loop, simply drag it into the workspace. It's automatically given its own track in the recording, as indicated by a thumbnail of the associated instrument. We're going to start with Euro Party Slicer FX, which runs for four bars. This obviously isn't going to be long enough for a whole song, so in the next step we'll adjust its length.

6. You can lengthen and shorten a loop by dragging on the ends of the sample, and needn't increase it so that it repeats in neat blocks of the full sample length if you only want to repeat a small portion. GarageBand loops have all been recorded in such a way that when you extend them the repeated opening portion runs off perfectly from the last few notes, effectively allowing you to repeat them infinitely.

7. We've set our sample to loop itself so that it fills up the existing track. We now need to add the other parts of our song by dragging them out from the loop selector. If you want to add more synth tracks, drag them out in the same way, and if you're starting to get familiar with the app you can use the search box at the top of the dialogue to hunt out any specific clips you want to incorporate.

We don't want to add any further synth tracks at this time; instead we want to work with another instrument. Tapping *Instrument*, however, only takes us back to the synth selector, so before doing this you need to tap *Reset Keywords* before *Instrument* to view the complete collection.

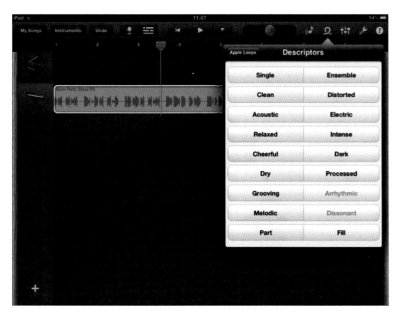

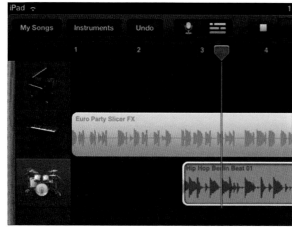

8. We've opened the drum loops. There are plenty to choose from, and as yet we haven't dragged one into our composition. That's because we need to filter the selection until it contains only those examples that would work well with the other parts of our composition already in place. Therefore, we've tapped the loops dialogue's *Descriptors* line, and will now tap *Processed* to filter only those loops that feature this style or effect.

9. Applying a descriptor significantly reduced the number of drums that met our requirements, making it easy to find one that worked well with the synth track that was already in place. Having auditioned each of the results we settled on Hip Hop Berlin Beat 01 and dragged it into the workspace. We want this to cut in after the first cycle of the synth loop, so we've positioned it so that its opening beat, which you can see indicated by the peaks and troughs in the soundwave, lines up with the first note after the second break in the synth track. We've played it back a few times to make sure the two are in sync.

10. Our track is really coming on now, and we're building up a complex composition by multi-layering our samples, even though we're not necessarily an experienced musician. You needn't be a singer, either, as GarageBand also includes loops of professionally-recorded vocals. As you can see from this grab, we've added a vocal that we've set to start before our synth and drum tracks by dragging both of them to the right and then dropping in our voice track. To accomplish this, as the original synth track was set to loop until it filled its track we have extended the section length of this part of our song by tapping the '+' on the timeline and then swiping up on the *Manual* setting.

11. With a synth, drums and now two vocal tracks, our song is starting to sound like the finished product. However, with so much else going on our vocal tracks are starting to get drowned out by the music that surrounds them. We'll fix this by reducing the volume of the synth. By default the volume controls are hidden, so pull out the sidebar to its full width by holding on the grab-handle on its right-hand edge and swiping into the workspace to reveal the controls. Drag the volume slider until the synth volume is more appropriate to accommodate the other parts of the track. You can mute it entirely by tapping the crossed-out speaker.

12. The one thing our track is still missing is a compelling beat that will tie together all of the other parts of the composition. Although we have dropped in a pre-recorded drum loop at parts we want to highlight, we also want to record our own additional drum track that will run through the whole of the song. Tap '+' to add a new track, then switch back to the instruments and scroll through until you get to *Drums*. Tap it to select.

13. GarageBand now presents you with a complete drum kit. You can switch between different kit styles – each with an appropriate sound of its own – by tapping the *Classic Studio Kit* button at the top of the screen.

    We're happy with this selection, so after a little rehearsal we're ready to add our self-drummed track to the song. Having made sure that the progress marker is at the start of the track, we tap the toolbar record button and start playing our drums in time to the pre-recorded part of our composition, which will play in the background. The composition will loop around, while a metronome keeps time in the background.

14. Switching back to the track organiser we can see that our drum track is now in place in a track of its own, with dotted highlights showing where our beats fall. This allows us to drag it around as we did with the other tracks so that each beat lines up with a significant part of our pre-recorded loops. We can also change the volume, as we did with the synthesiser track.

    We can add as many bespoke tracks of this kind as we like, including our own vocal tracks, allowing us to build up a unique composition using nothing more complex than an iPad with its built-in mic.

    All we need to do now is apply a little processing to our composition, to give it a professional finish.

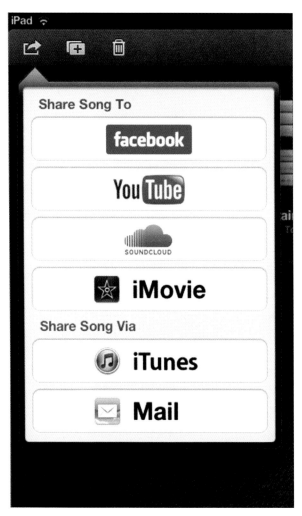

15. We'll do this by passing selected tracks through the Audio Recorder. Select the track you want to process and double-tap its icon in the sidebar. We can now play back the track and apply a selection of effects by tapping them on the right of the screen. Here we are applying the Telephone effect to our vocal track.

    With our track finished, we return to the track arranger, and then tap *My Songs* to return to the GarageBand file manager, from which we can share them to a variety of social networks or with friends (by emailing them) or sending them to iTunes.

Using iTunes U

iTunes U lets you put your iPad to use as an interactive learning tool through which you can access the very best courses from some of the world's top universities… all for free.

Apple has long been a favourite in education. Whether it's students using its computers to do their homework or schools kitting our their IT labs with MacBooks and iMacs to take advantage of their legendary reliability, ease of use, stability and longevity, it's a highly admired brand.

It increased its appeal yet further with the launch of iBooks Author (see *p138*), which has been designed specifically to make it easy for publishers to produce interactive books for use in education.

However, to focus purely on that new development would be to miss a long-standing educational resource that Apple first announced in 2007: iTunes U. The U, somewhat predictably, stands for University.

Introducing iTunes U

When Apple unveiled iTunes U on 30 May 2007, it described it as a service for creating, managing and distributing audio, video and file-based content for students. That doesn't sound entirely exciting, and the service was a bit fragmented, being hived off into a section of the iTunes Store, rather than being allowed to take centre stage.

However, over the next few years more and more institutions signed up so that by the beginning of 2012 more than 1000 universities and colleges were using iTunes U to distribute their content, both to students and the general public. In total, the combined catalogue now comprises over 500,000 pieces of audio and video, which

Apple claims makes iTunes the world's biggest repository of downloadable educational material. It's little wonder that in its first four years of operation it served over 700 million downloads.

With such a valuable educational resource to call upon, it was only natural that iTunes U would make Apple's hardware – and particularly its portable devices – even more appealing to students.

iTunes U improved

Apple capitalised on this when Apple launched iBooks Author by simultaneously revamping iTunes U, and giving it a dedicated application. This meant it was no longer necessary to download disparate pieces of media through the regular iTunes interface; instead you had a centralised location through which to search for, sign up to and work through free online courses.

The iTunes U app looks very similar to the iBooks app, with course material gathered together into bundles that look like regular books lined up on a familiar wooden bookshelf. There's even a catalogue that closely resembles what you might expect to see in the iBookstore.

Over the next three pages we'll show you how to find and sign up to free courses online, how to access the bundled material, and how to complete your assignments. If you aren't actually enrolled at an educational establishment you won't earn any qualifications, but it is a neat way to improve your overall knowledge and go back to education without paying a small fortune.

Signing up to your first course

1. Open the iTunes U app and tap the *Catalog* button at the top of the screen. The app flips around in the same way as iBooks to reveal the course guide. From here you can search using a topic or keyword, or use the charts which list both the top individual courses and top collections that users have been taking part in. Here, we're going to pick a course from the charts.

2. Just like a book from the iBookstore, or an album from the regular iTunes Store, each course in the listing is accompanied by a short description and a rating from other users. Here, we're looking at a course from Standford University on iPad and iPhone App Development, which has received high ratings. Having read through its description, we'll download it by tapping *Subscribe Free*.

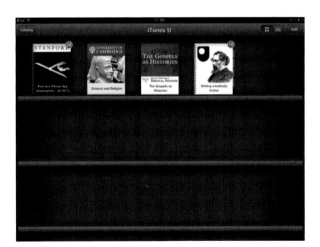

3. The new course will be added to your iTunes U shelves and is now ready for you to follow. Note how a blue notification badge on one corner of its cover indicates that there is new material waiting for you to access on the course. If any updates are delivered by the educational institution while you have the course installed, this is where you'll be told about them.

4. iTunes U courses are more than just a collection of audio, video and written files. Instead they are a collection of streamed and downloaded media, associated documents and written communications from the course leader. To help you keep track of each element of the course, they're organised in a virtual binder with tabs and menus for navigation. We'll explore this over the page.

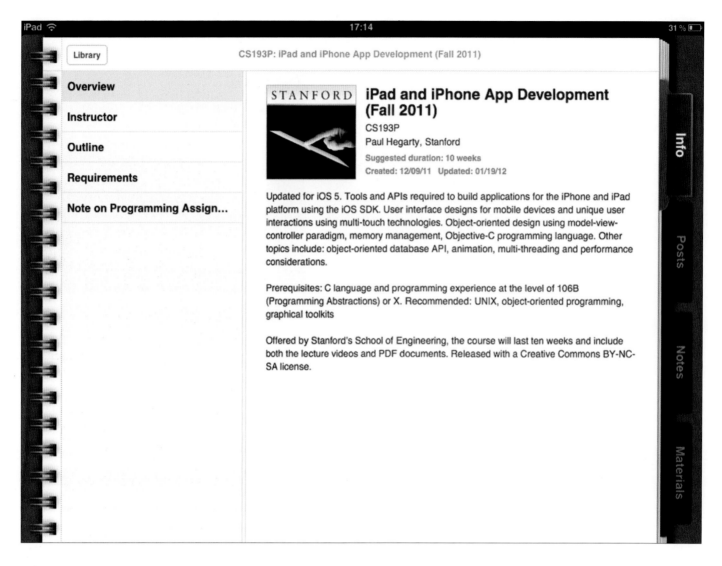

Understanding the course binder

The course binder is the container for all of the material that comprises your course. On first downloading the material, you should review the various sections on the Info page (you can return to this page at any point by tapping the *Info* tab). This gives you an outline of what you'll be learning, tells you some more about the tutor leading the course and, crucially, informs you of any requirements.

Often these will not be physical requirements such as a specific piece of equipment (although for this course you'd obviously need a computer capable of running Xcode, Apple's development environment for iOS applications), but also skill requirements. To follow this code on iPad and iPhone app development, for example,

the requirements are 'C language and programming experience at the level of 106B (Programming Abstractions) or X. Recommended: UNIX, object-oriented programming, graphical toolkits'.

Review each section of the introduction to ensure this is the course for you and you have the relevant qualifications to follow along, and then use the tabs to explore the rest of the material on offer. Bear in mind that at this stage the binder will probably be little more than just that: a device for holding material, much of which you won't yet have downloaded. These are detailed in the *Materials* section. Note that some of these may be charged for, as they could be course books that need to be downloaded from the iBookstore.

Accessing your course material

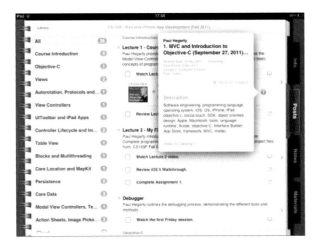

1. To save you downloading a lot of material in one go, all of the course material, accessible through the *Materials* tab, is set out in the *Posts* section. This breaks down the course into individual lectures, with the material for each one detailed in each section. Tap one of the grey bars to open a review of each content type, and the '*i*' button for a pop-up of further details.

2. One of the best things about learning through iTunes U is that it gives you access to high quality lecture videos, which look great on the iPad screen. Here we're watching the first lecture in the iPad and iPhone App Development course. Note that the transport bar at the bottom of the screen, which controls playback and volume, has a 30-second jump back button, for use if you miss anything.

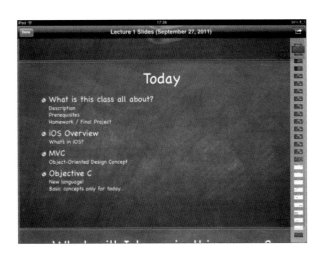

3. In many cases, the videos will be accompanied by a pack of slides, as used by the tutor when giving the lecture. These will often be posted to the course materials, allowing you to review the content of the video in your own time without having to run through it at the lecturer's pace – ideal for those unfamiliar with the material and getting to grips with a new topic or subject.

4. When you have completed each part of the course by watching a video, listening to audio, reading through course materials or reviewing lecture slides, you can tick it off by tapping on the check box beside its name in the Posts section. This helps you track your progress, but note that as you can jump backwards and forwards, these checks are only for your personal reference.

How to create your own iPad books

Apple's free iBooks Author application makes it easy to produce impressive, interactive digital books for reading on the iPad and selling through the iBookstore. Here, we show you how to put one together.

When Apple announced iBooks Author, alongside iBooks 2, the update to its e-reading software for the iPad, iPhone and iPod touch, it claimed it would revolutionise textbook publishing. Clearly it had done its homework and already convinced many professionals – teachers and publishers alike – that its vision was a viable one, as the glossy promotional video on its website contained plenty of impressive endorsements.

The software itself is free, and can be downloaded from the OS X App Store. That means, of course, that it won't run on an iPad, PC, nor on an older Mac with a PowerPC processor. This is a clever move on Apple's part, as iBooks Author not only heightens the iPad's appeal to those developing academic ebooks, but also helps it sell more Macs to the publishing industry.

iBooks Author follows very similar lines to Apple's office suite, iWork, with templates to get you started (*right*), and a simple drag-and-drop workflow once you start working on your book. This means you don't need to spend hours working out how your book should flow before you start putting in your content, and allows even non-technical, non-trained designers to work on the layout of their own book in the knowledge that they'll produce impressive results.

However, it's not without its limitations. Because you are always working with a template it's easy to produce books that look very similar to others built using iBooks Author. As we'll show you in this section, though, each is incredibly flexible, allowing you to change their layouts,

resize their placeholder images and reformat their sample text until you've created something that more accurately reflects the subject about which you're writing.

iBooks Author documents don't follow regular ePub conventions. Apple has, instead, mixed existing ePub standards, some unratified elements and its own extensions to produce very impressive results. Again, though, this introduces one very serious limitation: the number of platforms on which you can publish. iBooks Author books can only be read on an iPad. They are designed specifically for its 9.7in screen, and because of the extensions used in their underlying code you won't be able to port them to a third-party e-reading device. Your only choices if you want to address other devices are therefore to export your pages as PDF documents from within the application, or to start the work all over again – from scratch – in an alternative application to produce an open ePub version.

The final limitation comes in what you can do with your finished product. If you want to give it away – for free – then you needn't worry: you can do this whenever and wherever you want. However, the terms of the End User License Agreement (EULA) clearly state that if you want to make money from your work using its native format then separate rules apply:

"... if the work is provided for free (at no charge), you may distribute it by any means; if the work is provided for a fee (including as part of any subscription-based product or service) and includes files in the .ibooks format generated using iBooks Author,

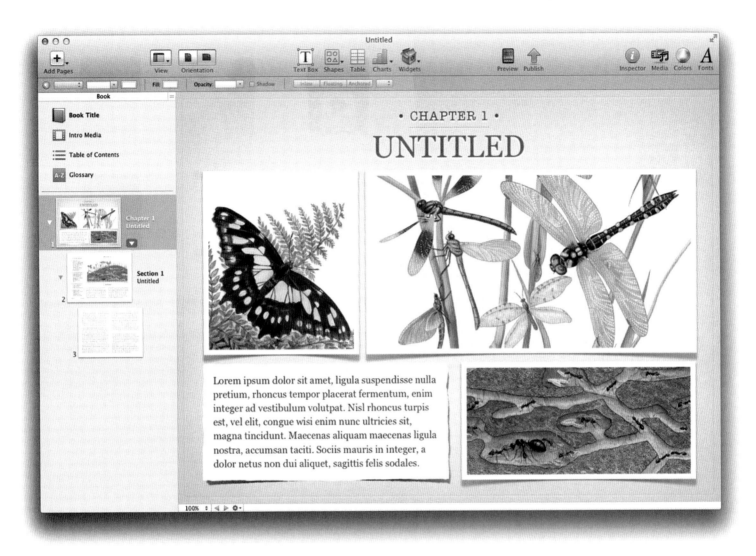

the work may only be distributed through Apple, and such distribution will be subject to a separate written agreement with Apple (or an Apple affiliate or subsidiary); provided, however, that this restriction will not apply to the content of the work when distributed in a form that does not include files in the .ibooks format generated using iBooks Author."

What does this mean? If you intend to charge for your book you can *only* sell it through the Apple iBookstore unless you first export it in text or PDF format.

Is this fair? That depends on your point of view. If you had invested hundreds of pounds in buying Adobe InDesign or QuarkXPress and either of those companies said that you could only sell your printed products through its own online stores, you'd cry foul – as many are doing about the iBooks Author license terms. However, iBooks Author is free. It's purely a tool for producing books that work on Apple's mobile devices and nothing else, in which case you could argue that it's entirely logical that Apple should restrict the distribution of its output in the same way that it regulates the distribution of iPhone and iPad apps. They, too, are produced using free software – Xcode – that any member of Apple's developer community can download and use to earn themselves an income.

So long as you're willing to work within these limitations, though, there's simply no easier a way to make high quality, attractive, interactive books for the iPad, as we'll show you here.

Creating your first book

The first thing you'll see when you start iBooks Author is the Template Chooser (*see over*). Although each of the templates appears to be designed for a specific kind of book – Botany, Astronomy, Entomology and so on – the more important distinction appears below each cover, where it describes the *kind* of book you can create with each one.

As iBooks Author is intended to be used for creating textbooks, we're going to steer clear of fiction and use it in this workthrough to produce a book for first-time chicken-keepers, for which the 'Craft' style will be most appropriate as its layouts are quite folksy and very approachable.

iBooks Author creates a sample book of three pages with some placeholder text and images on each one. We'll swap these out for our own content in the process of building our book.

If you have ever used Keynote or Pages then the iBooks Author interface will already look very familiar. For those who haven't used it, the toolbar's '*i*' button opens up the Inspector, which is where you'll do most of your formatting.

At the opposite end of the toolbar is the pilcrow (it looks like a backwards P), which is traditionally used to mark the end of a paragraph. This opens the styles drawer.

Although you can format each item of text individually using the font, size and spacing drop-down selectors on the toolbar, you should get into the habit of using styles to format your content so that you keep a consistent look and feel throughout your book, helping your readers to navigate the content and understand the various elements' hierarchical relationship to each other.

Adding and formatting content

The images and text that appear on the sample pages are placeholders, which you should swap out with your own content. At the moment they are only there to indicate the available boxes and to hold your styles. You can delete any of them that you don't want to use and resize them to fit a specific layout or the dimensions of their contents.

You can see layout of the default first page of our chosen craft template on the previous spread, and how we have flowed in our own text on this spread. You'll see we have removed two of the images, enlarged the one that remains and expanded the text box to match (*right*).

It's easy to keep your elements in line with one another as you drag and resize them on the page, as iBooks Author throws up dynamic guidelines that show when you have aligned their centre points or set their spacings to match. In the example on the facing page, the horizontal blue line shows that the image of the chicken we are dragging within the image block is centred on the vertical axis as the horizontal centres of the box and image align. Further, the blue marks between the 'chapter 1' and 'introduction' line, and between 'introduction' and the image indicate that the spaces between each element are the same. Matching your spacing in this way creates a more balanced, pleasing layout. Further feedback is given

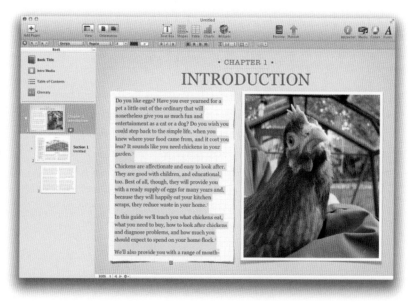

• CHAPTER 1 •

INTRODUCTION

Do you like eggs? Have you ever yearned for a pet a little out of the ordinary that will nonetheless give you as much fun and entertainment as a cat or a dog? Do you wish you could step back to the simple life, when you knew where your food came from, and it cost you less? It sounds like you need chickens in your garden.

Chickens are affectionate and easy to look after. They are good with children, and educational, too. Best of all, though, they will provide you with a ready supply of eggs for many years and,

in the pop-up coordinates that move with the pointer to show the image's precise position on the page.

The Inspector

The Inspector is where you'll make most of your choices. It's split into sections to cater for each part of your document, allowing you to make significant changes to every aspect of your document. In the grab to the left we are using the Text Inspector to reformat our text by tweaking character size, colour and so on.

Whenever you make a change in this way, it stops the selected text from conforming to its assigned style. Although it does nothing to stop you from doing this, iBooks Author does throw up a warning in the shape of a red triangle beside the style name in the styles drawer. Clicking this calls up a menu through which you can tell it how to handle the aberration. If you want to preserve the original formatting so that you can reuse it, you would opt to '*Create Paragraph Style from selection*'. This would effectively preserve the original settings while allowing you to apply the new style again elsewhere.

However, we want to change the style itself, so on this occasion we are selecting '*Redefine Style from Selection*' (*right*). By changing the style in this way the current formatting will ripple through the rest of the document, with all

other sections formatted in line with the same style being restyled to match. This is the power of working with styles: they are an efficient and effective time-saver when it comes to implementing changes to formatted text.

Now that we're happy with how the page looks we'll delete the other pages in the chapter by right-clicking the second page in the sidebar and selecting *Delete Section*. With this done we can now go on to perform a very important design process: handling what should happen when the iPad is rotated.

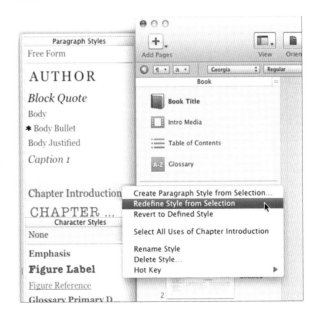

Looking both ways

Because our book is so precisely designed, with positioned boxes, images and copy in the place of simple flowing text, we need to consider what will happen when our readers turn their iPad around from landscape to portrait orientation. As it stands, our book is only designed for use on a landscape display.

Click the toolbar's portrait orientation button to switch to the alternate view and see how it affects your document. In our case it breaks our design. Our chicken image disappears and the text is left dangling off the bottom of the page. We'll fix this before we continue.

We'll do this by copying the chicken image from the landscape layout by clicking back to it on the toolbar, selecting the image and using command-C to copy it to the clipboard. Switching back to portrait we then use command-V to paste it on the page. We an now resize it and move it into its final position. As you can see from the image below, we have also rotated it slightly and have changed the size of its bounding box, having clicked *Edit Mask* to unlock its dimensions and then dragged the handles on each edge. Doing this also allows us to enlarge the image by using the slider.

Our first page is now complete, but before we go any further we should preview it in iBooks. To do this you'll need an connect your iPad to your Mac. Start iBooks 2 and click *Preview* on the iBooks Author toolbar. Select your iPad in the dialogue box that drops down and the book will be compiled and sent to your device.

There won't be much to look at right now as we have only created a single page document, but it's important to check that it works in both orientations by rotating the iPad through 90 degrees (*below*). Everything is working as we expected, so we can move on to the next part of our project.

Creating chapters

Our single-page introduction is our first chapter. We now need to add chapters for our remaining content, each of which will be multi-page sections.

We do this by clicking *Add Pages | Chapter | Chapter*. iBooks Author drops a new untitled chapter into the sidebar, again consisting of a single page. If you're following along with your own copy of iBooks Author you'll immediately appreciate one of the limitations we discussed earlier: the fact that iBooks Author's limited templates means your books can become quite samey.

The new chapter that has been added to our book opens with the same layout as the introduction did before we started working on it. Fortunately, though, since we have made considerable changes to the layout of the introduction our readers shouldn't spot that. To make sure, though, we'll go further and redesign this chapter to give it a more appropriate layout, and a look and feel all of its own, first by amending this opening page, and then by tweaking the pages that follow.

Working with images

Images really bring your work to life, not only breaking up the text so that reading it doesn't seem such a daunting prospect, but also helping to illustrate your points.

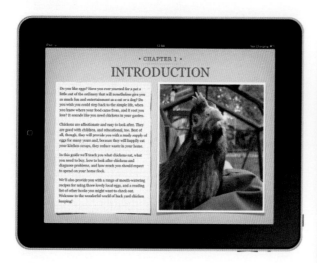

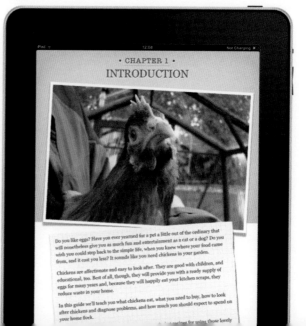

You can drag images into your layouts in either landscape or portrait mode, although the end result will be slightly different, depending on which method you choose.

Landscape mode

Drag in an image in landscape orientation and you can anchor it precisely by moving the blue dot that marks its position within the text. The text will reflow around it as you change its position. It should be noted, though, that an image's anchor position doesn't necessarily relate to its position on the page. You can independently move the image within the layout; the spot merely ties the image to your other content so that should the content be shunted onto another page as you change the copy the image reference will move with it.

Portrait mode

In portrait mode, images are lined up in the sidebar. Once they've been transferred to the iPad, tapping these thumbnails opens larger versions in a new window. However, you can't position your images as precisely in this mode as you can in landscape mode, as they only ever line up with the references in the flowing text.

Placing your images in portrait mode adds a number of further elements that aren't appended automatically when placing images in landscape mode, including a caption and figure reference. These are not included automatically when positioning them in landscape mode, but can be added by selecting the image in that orientation and opening the Widget Inspector.

Here, you can select whether or not to display the title above the image, the caption below it and a background behind it. Setting the margin dimensions lets you control how close the surrounding text comes to it when it's flowing around its edges.

Creating a cohesive product

As you flow in your text, iBooks Author creates as many pages as required to contain it. By default these are plain text pages, but you can drop images into them or change the template by clicking the down-pointing arrow to the right of the page and selecting an alternative style.

Although the pages are arranged vertically in the sidebar, once they are transferred to an iPad your readers will move from one to the next by sweeping them to one side. The main editing window, therefore, arranges your pages in the same way. Should your monitor be large enough to allow it, drag out the iBooks Author window to display as many pages as you can (*below*) so that you can see how the pages interact with each other and ensure there are no jarring contrasts that will only manifest themselves as your readers navigate the finished book.

Working with widgets

So far you might be wondering why Apple was so sure that iBooks Author would revolutionise textbooks. It makes books easy to lay out, and produces attractive results, but until you start working with widgets other than plain images you're probably wondering what all the fuss is about.

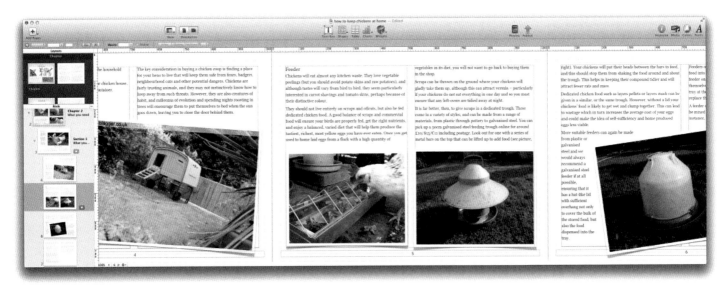

There are seven different widgets to choose from (*right*), each of which helps to promote self-guided learning. They are largely self-explanatory, with *Media* handling video and audio, *3D* taking care or rotatable objects, and *Keynote* exposing a box in which you can place an existing Keynote presentation, allowing you to create slide-based content in Apple's answer to Microsoft PowerPoint and incorporate it in your book if you find this an easier way to work. We want to introduce an image gallery into our book, so we'll start by selecting Gallery from the Widgets menu.

Every Widget can be customised courtesy of the Widget Inspector. We have therefore positioned our Gallery widget at the end of the first chapter and selected *Top* from the list of layout options. This moves all of the associated titles and captions above the image itself and therefore positions the image immediately above the navigation dots.

That's the bare bones of our widget in place. However, it currently doesn't have any content. We need to add some pictures, which we do by switching to the Inspector's Interaction tab and using the '+' button to add images from the OS X file system. We have added seven pictures, which is about perfect as it's not too many for our readers to wade through, but in reality you can add far more as the pane is a scrolling window, and the currently displayed image is indicated below the widget by a spot (*below*).

Should you prefer, you can replace these dots with thumbnails that switch out the images as your readers tap them. You can also change the order in which the images are presented by dragging the three bars that appear to the right of each one in the Gallery Media pane (*above*).

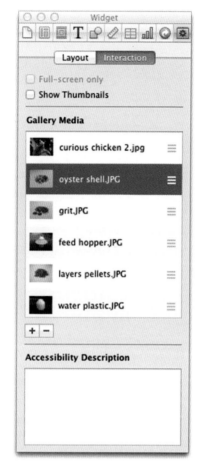

Each image needs an associated caption, which will be switched out in sync with the pictures as your reader taps through them. Click through each image in the Inspector's Gallery Media pane and replace the placeholder text on your page above it with the caption that explains its contents. This description can either repeat content from the main body of your work or add something new, but whatever you choose to put bear in mind that any reader browsing through your book should be able to get something out of it without having read the rest of the spread on which it appears. You should therefore, consider the caption to be an opportunity to present a summary of the text to which it relates, so leading the reader into the page. When your gallery appears in the finished book, those reading the book in landscape orientation can swipe through its various elements in situ (*left*). Readers with a portrait-oriented iPad will find the gallery in the sidebar, like a regular image. Tapping it there opens it full-screen and hides the rest of the book layout.

The Image Gallery is just one of the widgets on offer to editors working with iBooks Author. Despite the fact that it's fairly simple, doing no more than presenting images and captions, it is one of the many elements that won't translate well to regular ePub, and will have to be re-created as flat graphics for other platforms.

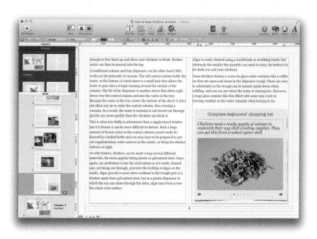

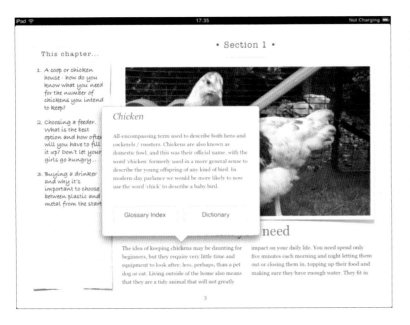

Building a glossary

If you are writing a technical manual, you should include a glossary of terms used throughout the book. iBooks 2 on the iPad has a specific Glossary entry in the navigation drop-down through which your readers can find definitions of the terms you have used in your book. Glossary entries also pop up in any searches performed.

The glossary is a special part of the book; scrolling to the top of the iBooks Author sidebar reveals this, the cover, opening media and contents page. Although you can tweak the contents manually, it is built automatically as you define various headings throughout your book. For the moment, then, we can ignore it.

Add each definition by clicking the '+' button in the sidebar and giving it a headword, then switch to the main body of the document and replace the placeholder text with your definition. Once you have defined several words you can start dragging related terms from the headwords column into the related area below your definition. These will be hyperlinked in the exported document so that tapping on any one of them takes your reader to the linked definition without them having to enter the word using the keyboard.

If you're still in the throes of editing your book then you can cut some time here by building your glossary as you work your way through the book. Turn on the Glossary Toolbar (click *View | Show Glossary Toolbar* or

press shift-command-E) and highlight the term you'd like to add to the glossary where it appears on your laid-out page. It will be automatically added to the Glossary toolbar, with an option to add it to the glossary at one end of the toolbar, and to link the word to an existing definition at the opposite end.

Choosing this latter option doesn't change the formatting of the word on the page, so decide whether you want to employ an easily recognised device along the same lines as a hyperlink to indicate to your readers that tapping on the link will pop up a definition bubble (*left*).

Publishing your product

It's important to keep saving and previewing your work on an iPad as you progress through your book so that you won't get to the end and find any nasty surprises. Once you've finished your layout it's time to think about how you want to make it available to the general public. You have three options here:

1. If you want to charge for it, click *Publish* on the iBooks Author toolbar to submit the book to the iBookstore. This will save a packaged version of the book that you can upload to the store using iTunes Producer. Bear in mind, though, that to go down this route you'll need an iBookstore seller account and an agreement in place covering your US tax obligations (even if you are located outside of the US, when you will want to opt out of having 30% tax deducted at source). You'll also have to create a sample of the book that your potential readers can download in advance of buying the complete product.

2. Export an iBooks file for loading onto an iPad to be read using iBooks 2 (click *File | Export*). Bear in mind that even though you're not going to be using the iBookstore the terms of the End User License Agreement still state that you can't sell the book, even through your own web site.

3. Export the book as a series of PDF pages (again, *File | Export*) that can be opened in a regular application on any platform, so are suitable for readers without an iPad. Since Apple updated its End User License Agreement, you can now sell books of this sort through other channels than the iBookstore.

Control iTunes remotely

Use your home network to wirelessly stream your tracks to – and control them from – your iPad, courtesy of Apple's free Remote application, which also works on the iPhone and iPod touch.

Not only does it produce the world's best-selling tablet – the iPad – its best-selling range of portable music players – the iPod – and one of its highest regarded mobile phones – the iPhone – but Apple is also proprietor of the world's largest online music store. This is intimately linked to iTunes, its own music playback application, which by association has itself become one of the most popular means of organising and playing tracks. With all of its products sharing several common features, it was therefore only natural that Apple should link them all together with a small application called Remote.

Available as a free download from the App Store (*bit.ly/xhEKCK*), Remote replicates much of the iTunes interface on your iPad, iPhone or iPod touch, allowing you to play on your iPad, tracks stored on your computer across your local network, or control the playback of those same tracks on your computer itself without

touching its keyboard or mouse. For anyone with AirPort Express hooked up to a set of speakers, this is a boon, as it means they can change what they're listening to from any room in their home.

Setting up Remote

Once you've installed Remote you need to give it authorisation to access your iTunes library. You can do this in two ways, either by turning on Home Sharing if this is already active on your computer-hosted library, or by adding the library manually (*below, left*).

If you're doing the former, you'll need to enter the Apple ID and password connected to your library, after which all of the libraries registered to that ID on your local network will appear in a menu (*below*). Tapping on one opens its contents in the Remote application window, ready to be controlled.

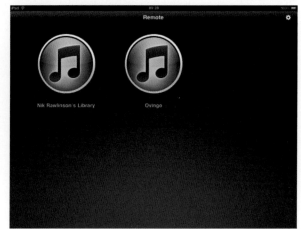

Setting it up without Home Sharing active is slightly more involved as it relies on pairing the library and application by entering a randomised four-digit code (*above*).

Tap Add an iTunes Library to get started, at which point your iPad will pop up in the iTunes sidebar on your computer. Click it here and copy the numbers from your iPad onto the screen (*above right*) to complete the pairing.

Using Remote

Now that your iPad and computer are paired you can control the computer from your tablet device.

The Remote interface looks very similar to the iOS Music app, with categories running down the left-hand sidebar and a menu of your media filling the largest part

of the window to the right of this. You can use the buttons at the bottom of the screen to reorganise them by album, artist, song and so on.

The regular transport buttons control your computer and the display at the top of the interface replicates whatever is showing in your regular iTunes application – not only those actions that you instigated from Remote.

If you have several different output sources, such as remote speakers connected by AirPort Express or Apple TV, these appear in a drop-down menu from the speaker icon (*see below*), allowing you to pick between them or select multiple speakers to address simultaneously.

Should you want to stop using Remote, you'll need to unpair it from your iTunes Library. To do this, select *Preferences...* | *Devices* on your computer and click the *Forget All Remotes* button. Complete the process by also deleting Remote from your iPad.

Find My Friends

With so many of us now carrying compatible iOS devices, Apple has made it easy for us to find one another thanks to their integrated Location Services features and a free-to-download application from the App Store: Find My Friends.

F ind My Friends is Apple's own people-locating application. It works on both the iPhone and iPad, and uses data from the cellphone network or wifi connection to plot another user on your device, allowing you to quickly and easily find where they are. It isn't installed by default, but it's a free download from the App Store at *bit.ly/zGd83b*. Once you've downloaded it, log in using your regular Apple ID credentials.

Clearly Apple couldn't put out this information without first gaining users' permission or it would risk being pulled up for invasion of privacy, so your first step is to send a message to your friends and ask them to allow you to see their location. They'll need an iOS device of their own for this to work.

Turn your iPad to landscape orientation and tap the '+' button at the top of the sidebar. Enter the name of the friend you want to find and, optionally, add a message of your own – particularly if you think they might not know what Find My Friends is all about (*see right*).

Apple will send them an email containing a link (*below*) which when tapped on an iOS device takes them to their own installed copy of Find My Friends so that they can accept or deny your request.

Each of your authorised friends will now appear in the Find My Friends sidebar, from where you can tap between them to view each person's location on a Google Map in either plan, satellite or hybrid view. A small badge beside their name shows how far they are from your current location (*opposite, top*), with a floating flag pinpointing their position.

At the bottom of the screen you'll see their current address (this may be an approximation rather than a specific door number and street name) and options to open their full contact information and directions from your position to theirs.

This final option drops you out of Find My Friends and into the Maps application, which plots the quickest routes by private vehicle, public transport or foot in the usual manner (*left*).

Find My Friends can also work in reverse, with you temporarily allowing contacts to see your location. This is particularly useful if, say, you're attending a trade show and your colleagues need to be able to find you at short notice. In this situation, tap the *Temporary* button on the toolbar at the foot of the interface and enter the contact details to which the invitation to see your location should be sent, along with an expiry date after which they won't be able to track you any longer.

Bear in mind that activating Location Services in this way can drain your battery more quickly than usual.

Parental Controls

The iPad is a great educational tool, and kids will take quickly to its tactile touch, sweep and pinch way of working. That's all the more reason for you to consider how to keep them safe when using the App Store and other downloaded content.

Apple has been slightly inconsistent when it comes to tailoring the specific abilities and content of an iPad, iPhone and iPod touch. If you want to keep your children away from content you feel is inappropriate for them, you should turn to Parental Controls in iTunes' Preferences on your Mac or PC (*right*), and to Restrictions on the iPad (*Settings | General | Restrictions*). Both of these let you exert increasing levels of control over what can be downloaded and installed, until you get to the point where you're happy allowing younger users to get their hands on your iPad.

To invoke restrictions on your iPad, tap *Enable Restrictions* and choose a four-digit security code (*below*). This must be entered when making any changes to your settings, and so should stop your children disabling them. Once restrictions are enabled you can disable whole applications, such as Safari, YouTube and iTunes, forbid

App Store installations (*1*) and switch off the location features.

Ratings can be tailored for specific territories, with options for Australia, Canada, France, Germany, Ireland, Japan, New Zealand, the UK and the US (*2*). Choosing your home territory will let you pick from restrictions that match your local ratings. So, pick UK and you'll have movie ratings of U, Uc, PG, 12, 12A, 15 and 18. Switch to Ireland, though, and you'll be able to choose from G, PG, 12, 15, 16 and 18 (*3*). Likewise, in the UK you can allow all or no TV shows, or just those rated for 'Caution' (*4*). In the US, though, you have 16 ratings from TV-Y to TV-MA. In all countries, the choices for podcasts are simply on or off for explicit content (*5*), but the options for applications are more extensive and match Apple's own App Store ratings system (*6*).

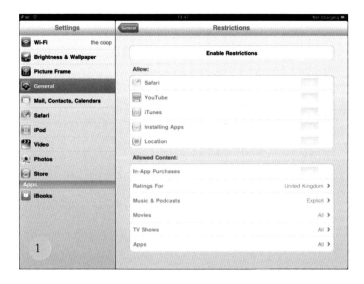

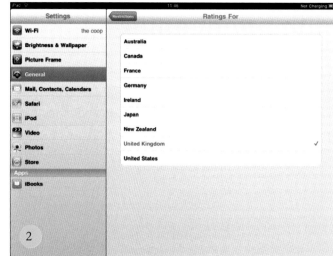

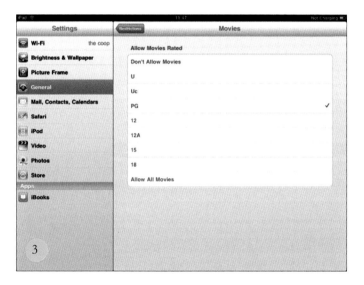

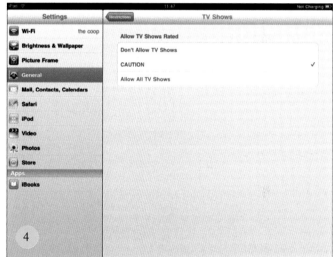

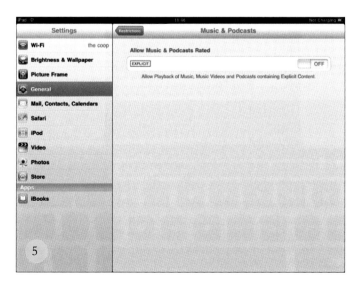

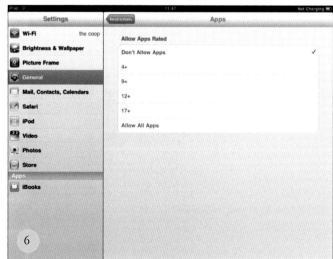

Set up your email

Keep in touch with friends, family and work colleagues wherever you happen to be by setting up your email using iOS and the iPad's excellent Mail app. Here we'll show you how to get started, and send your first few messages.

The iPad was the logical successor to Apple's phenomenally successful iPhone, so it's only natural that the two should share a lot of common features. Chief among them is email.

A big part of the iPhone's success is down to the significance of that initial 'i' which most take to relate to Internet, like the 'i' on iMac and the terminated iWeb. Not only has the iPhone long been a first class means of browsing the web, but it's also got a great built-in email client, which builds on the success of similar apps long shipped by rivals, by enabling users to get hold of their messages – and send replies or conversation openers – without first heading home or back to the office.

Obviously if you only have a wifi iPad, rather than a 4G-enabled device, you'll still only be able to send and receive email when connected to a wireless network or via a personal hotspot, as provided by the iPhone 4 (and later), and new iPad on some contracts. Whichever model you have, though, over the next four pages we'll show you how to get your email account set up to send and receive your first few messages.

Configuring your accounts

1. Tap *Settings | Mail, Contacts, Calendars*. You'll return to this part of iOS every time you need to make a change to your email accounts and various synchronised services, so it's well worth getting familiar with it. If you already have any accounts set up they'll be displayed here. If not, you'll be taken directly to the Add Account screen. If you don't see this right now, tap *Add Account...* to get started (see grab, *right*).

2. iOS has presets for a wide variety of different account types, including traditionally webmail-based options such as Gmail and Hotmail, corporate servers such as Exchange, and Apple's own services: iCloud and MobileMe. Note that iCloud is MobileMe's replacement, and that MobileMe will disappear over the next few months. Although the usernames, passwords and server addresses for each option will differ slightly, the principle is the same in each case. We'll set up a Gmail account over the next few steps.

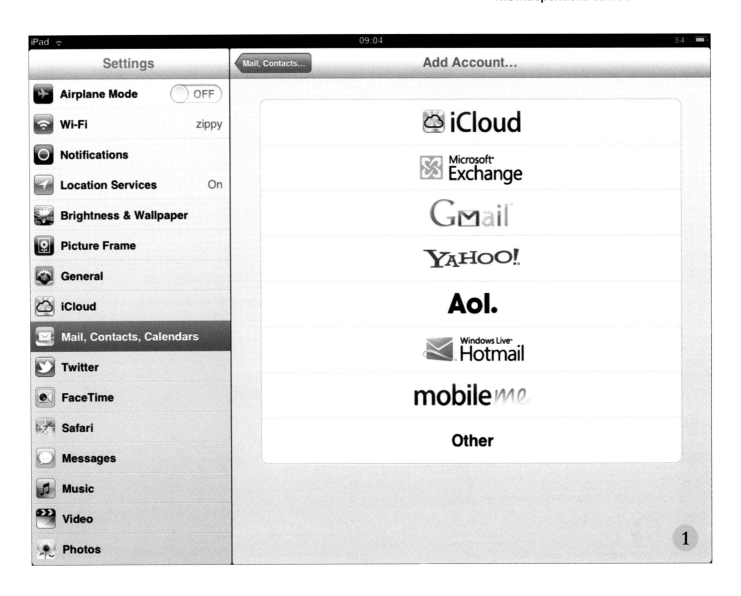

3. Tap the icon for the service you want to set up, and it'll pop up a panel containing only boxes for the information required (*left*). In this case, that's Name, Address and Password, plus a Description of the account to help us distinguish it.

   The name you enter will be used to brand all of your outgoing emails, so whatever you enter here is what your recipients see in the From fields in their email application, rather than your less friendly email address. The description, meanwhile, is only there so that you can specify how the account is identified on your iPad. You can therefore enter whatever works best for you. The Address and Password, however, are more important, as they are used to validate your access to the service.

4. iOS verifies your credentials and if they're accepted by the server it'll progress to the next step. This is where you choose which services you want to use. In many cases, your only option will be email, but in our case we can also use our Google account to keep track of our calendars and notes. We'll opt in to the first of those two, but not the second, and then tap Save to complete the process. (*overleaf*)

Quick Tip

As well as setting up your email accounts, this is also the place to head when you want to set up synchronisation with a shared calendar or an online address book using LDAP or CardDAV.

5. We're going to add another email account now, this
    time using a domain that we own ourselves. The first
    part of the process is the same, requiring that we open
    Settings | Mail, Contacts, Calendars and then tap *Add
    Account...* before entering our regular login credentials.

6. Because we're not using a preset service, we need to
    tell iOS a bit more about the protocols it should use
    to connect to the server and download our email. In
    this case we're using IMAP, which is a convention that
    synchronises our local mailboxes with the ones held
    on the server. That means that when we read a
    message on our iPad it'll also be marked as read both
    on the server and inside any other clients that are
    accessing the same account on other devices. Further,
    any messages we send from our device will be copied
    back to the server, and from there downloaded to our
    other clients. This means we can be sure that whatever
    device we're using to manage our email will always be
    in sync with any others we may own, so we'll have no
    trouble finding our data. Plus, as a bonus, our sent and
    read messages will be safely archived somewhere other
    than our iPad, which only keeps a small number of
    messages in its mailboxes at any one time. If we
    instead chose POP, the messages would still download
    in the same way, but there would be no
    synchronisation with the server, so no other client
    application would know if we had read the message
    somewhere else, nor have a record of our outgoing
    messages sent from elsewhere.

7. Although our iPad knows what our email address is, it
    doesn't know how to collect our messages as we're not
    using one of the pre-set services. We'll therefore scroll
    down to the Incoming Mail Server section and enter
    the details we have sourced from our ISP, giving the
    server address, our user name and a password. As
    with the pre-set account types, iOS will check these
    credentials with the server as part of the set-up
    process to make sure that they're valid. Further down
    the panel we also need to provide details of an
    outgoing mail server, again using the information
    provided by our ISP. Once we have, tapping *Next*
    verifies our settings and completes the process.

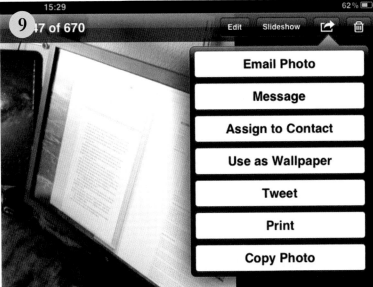

Sending your first message

Now that your accounts are set up, you're ready to start sending and receiving your first messages. Close the Preferences app and open Mail. In the iPad's default configuration, this is found on the springboard.

8. Any messages already waiting for you on the server will be immediately downloaded and dropped into your inbox. (Check our full section on using Mail starting on p34 for more on dealing with these.) At this point we just want to send a message, so tap the new message icon at the top of the toolbar and start typing.

9. Although the iOS Mail app has no problem sending images, you can't attach them directly from within the application itself. Instead you need to take them from the Photos app. There are two options here: either sending them directly or copying them across. To send photos directly, navigate to the image you want to send and tap the shortcut button (the box with the arrow swooping out of it) then select the option to send by email. The image will be attached to a message and you'll be able to select the size you want to send it at. It makes sense to not send the full size image if you really don't need to as it will take longer to dispatch and consume more of your recipient's inbox (possibly pushing them over their account limit if they have a set quota) and if you are using a cell-based network over 3G or 4G or a personal hotspot the bandwidth consumed by larger images will be deducted from your data allowance. Note that emailing an image this way only works if you want to start a new message containing the picture.

10. If you are already in the midst of composing your email, you can instead copy the image across in the same way that you would copy typed data between applications. Simply hold down on the image within the Photos app until the action bar pops up, and then select *Copy*. Now switch back to your message and hold down again at the point where you would like to drop the image and, when the bar pops up, select *Paste* to add it to your message.

Find a lost iPad

Should you become parted from your iPad, increase your chances of being reunited with the help of iCloud's Find My iPad service, which locates it on a map and either locks or wipes it remotely.

Apple recognises that as many of us take our iPad everywhere we go, there's always a chance we could lose it. This might be completely innocent, as we could leave it on the bus or in the back of a taxi, or it could be more malicious with our gadgets stolen from our bags.

However you happen to be parted from your iPad, though, you want the best chance possible of finding it again or, if it's been taken dishonestly, at least removing all of your data to keep it safe from prying eyes.

That's where Find My iPad comes in. Originally developed to calm business users' worries, and put off thieves, it's a boon for consumers.

What is Find iPad

Find My iPad is a smart service that uses iCloud to locate your iPad anywhere in the world using its GPS chip or an active wifi connection.

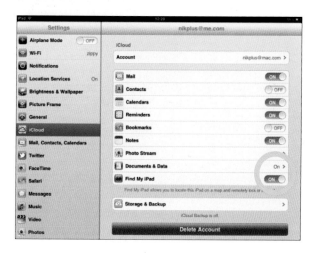

It relies on you having at least one iCloud email account active on the device, which is set to receive push email. If you don't get have this set up, tap *Settings | Mail, Contacts, Calendars | Add Account...* and select iCloud from the list of account type options.

Activate Find My iPad

Find My iPad is turned off by default. This makes sense as it relies on passing your current location through the iCloud servers, which some users may consider to be a security risk. To turn it on, tap *Settings | iCloud* and tap the ON/OFF slider beside Find My iPad (*left*).

Log in to your account at *icloud.com* using a regular browser and click the icon in the top left corner to open the iCloud apps menu. Select *Find My iPhone*.

Right away iCloud starts searching for each of the devices that you've registered to your account and plotting them on a map. You can switch between them by clicking each one in the *My Devices* panel, and switch between zoomable map, satellite and hybrid views to help you zoom in to the closest possible location.

Select the device that you need to locate – in our case an iPad – and it will be highlighted on the map with a small pop-up bubble protruding from a pushpin. Clicking the blue '*i*' at the end of the bubble gives you three options for remotely controlling your device: sending a message, remotely locking it and wiping it completely.

Your first step should always be to send a message, which will be immediately displayed on the screen when your iPad next connects to the net.

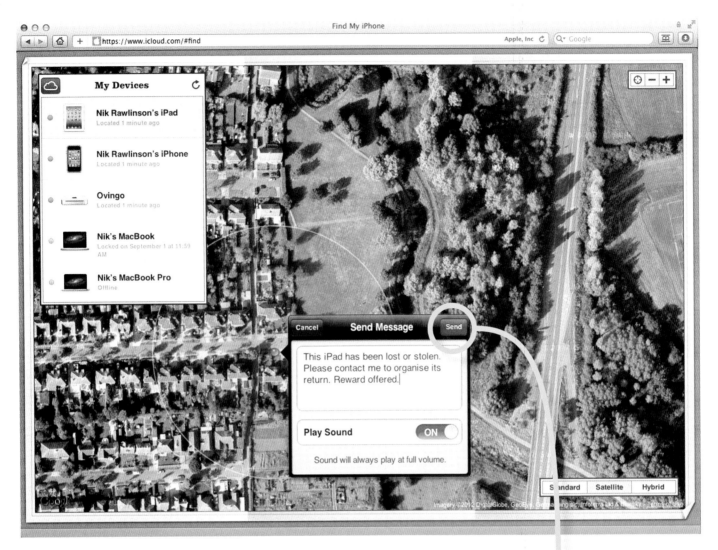

Include in this message whatever details would help facilitate the return of your iPad, but be careful not to give away too many personal details or put yourself at risk by organising a meeting in unsafe circumstances. By default iCloud will have set the option to play a sound at the same time as displaying the message.

If this doesn't yield a successful result then you should move on to the next steps: either locking it or wiping it.

When locked, the iPad can only be unlocked using your existing security code. If you have set your iPad to wipe after 10 unsuccessful entries then you already have another level of security built in. Your last line of defence is the remote wipe carried out directly through *icloud.com*. You should only do this if you're sure that you're not going to get your iPad back as it's impossible to locate it again using Find My iPad once it's been wiped.

Above: Alert whoever happens to be using your iPad to the fact that it's been lost or stolen by sending a message to the screen. This will be displayed, along with an uncomfortable, loud beeping, until they acknowledge it by tapping OK, so it's impossible for them to claim that they didn't know the device's status. Always take care when arranging for the return of a lost or stolen iPad and agree a meeting in a public place. Never put yourself in a position of risk or danger.

Glossary

The iPad is a supremely friendly piece of kit, but the world it inhabits is populated by unfamiliar words and acronyms. Here are some of the most common terms you'll come across in daily iPad use.

AAC

Advanced Audio Codec (AAC) is the preferred format for music storage in iTunes and on the iPad. It is also the standard format for music tracks (although not Podcasts) downloaded from the iTunes Music Store. It can be converted to MP3 for greater cross-platform compatibility.

AIFF

Audio Interchange File Format, developed by Apple in 1988 and most commonly used on its range of Mac desktop and laptop computers.

Album Art

Iconised versions of album and single covers downloaded automatically at the same time as music bought from the iTunes Store. This is displayed in a pane on the iTunes interface, on the screens of iPods (except iPod shuffle) and, of course, the iPad, during track playback. Album art can also be added to tracks you have ripped yourself, either by scanning the artwork or by tasking an application such as CoverScout to source them for you from the web.

Apple ID

Account used by Apple to tie together all of your various interactions with its online services, including the iTunes Store, App Store, iBookstore and iCloud. It also takes care of your credit card details so you don't need to enter them every time you make a purchase.

Audiobooks

Specially formatted audio files (not necessarily books) that allow for bookmarking. Stopping playback of an audiobook track at any point will save your position so that when you resume playing the next time you'll pick up at the same place.

Bit rate

Means of expressing the number of audio samples processed in a set period of time, usually a second. See also KBPS.

Capacity

The amount of data that can be held by your iPad. This will be slightly smaller than the stated capacity of the iPad itself due to the way capacities are measured and space consumed by iOS. To find out how much of your iPad's

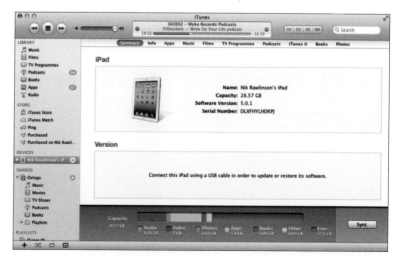

available capacity you have consumed, tap *Settings | About*, or select your iPad in the iTunes sidebar on your Mac or PC where a colour-coded bar shows not only how much of your available capacity you have used up, but what kind of data is filling the space (*below left*).

Dock

Small brick-like device with a slot for the iPad to sit in. Inside the slot is a connector that exactly matches that on the end of an iPad data cable. Bundled with first-generation iPads, but now an optional extra. Sitting the iPad in the Dock both charges it and updates its contents. Apple produces two Docks for the iPad, with one sporting an integrated keyboard, which turns the iPad into a compact desktop computer for daily use.

DRM

Digital Rights Management. A range of software-based systems that control how digital content can be used and how many times it can be copied. It protects music creators' and publishers' copyrights. Now largely less restrictive than it once was.

FairPlay

The DRM system used by iTunes and the associated Music Store. It is used to protect some AAC-encoded audio files and was, some say, key to the success of the

iPod, as only iTunes-compatible players such as the iPod could play back FairPlay-protected music tracks.

GB

Shorthand for gigabyte. Roughly one billion bytes, where one byte is equivalent to a single character, such as the letter 'a' stored on a disk. It is a measurement of data capacity, and is the terminology used when describing the capacity of the iPad.

H.264

High quality digital video format that allows videos to be highly compressed while retaining as high a quality as possible. Widely used by Apple and YouTube, and likely to become more popular with mass adoption of HTML5.

iCloud

Online service that has replaced MobileMe. It offers both web-based and client-based email, an online calendar and data synchronisation and backup, allowing you to share iWork documents between iOS devices and photos between iOS devices and iPhoto on your Mac (*left*).

Imap

Internet Message Access Protocol: a standard used for handling email that synchronises messages between the server and the client device. As a result, any messages that you send will not only be saved on the device on which you create them, but also copied to the server and, from there, synchronised to any other device that also has access to that email account.

iMovie

Consumer-grade movie editing software. It started life on the Mac but is now also available on the iPad and iPhone, allowing for editing on the move. Handles pictures, sound and transitions in a user-friendly interface.

iOS

Operating system that underpins the iPad, iPhone and iPod touch and bundles together both the firmware that interacts with the hardware inside the device and the core applications, such as Safari and Mail. Formerly called iPhone OS, and sharing many of the underlying code of OS X, the operating system that runs the Mac.

incorporates an address book, music and video player, mapping application and full-blown email client, with push-email services similar to those found on a Blackberry communications device.

iPhoto

Consumer-level photo management and editing application, which forms part of Apple's creativity suite, iLife. It can now be bought separate from the other apps in the suite. As well as being an iOS application, the Mac version is the eventual archival destination for all images synchronised from your iPad, iPhone or iPod touch using Photo Stream.

iPod

As well as a generic term used to describe Apple's range of portable music players and the equivalent playback software on the iPhone and iPad it is, more specifically, how Apple describes the full-sized, top-end player in its range, now called the classic. The closest equivalent to the iPhone and iPad is the multitouch-enabled iPod touch, which can also run many iOS apps.

iPhone

All-in-one communications and entertainment device from Apple, produced as a follow-up to its phenomenally successful iPod line of portable music players. It was developed amid utmost secrecy, and finally revealed to the public in January 2007, following massive blog and media speculation. As well as regular telephony features, it

iTunes

Apple software for both PCs and Macs used to download, store and play back music, interact with its own online music store and transfer tracks and data to and from an iPad. On the iPad it is used entirely for downloads and management, not for media playback.

iWork

Office suite comprising Pages (word processor), Numbers (spreadsheet) and Keynote (presentation application, *left*), which generally correspond to Microsoft's Word, Excel and PowerPoint. It started life on the Mac and to date has not appeared on Windows for PC users, but each of the applications has now been ported to iOS where they run on both the iPad and the iPhone / iPod touch. The iOS editions of each application use iCloud to synchronise documents across multiple devices.

Kbps

Kilobits per second. A measurement of the number of audio samples that go to make up each second of music in a digitally-encoded track. The higher this number, the smoother the file that will be reproduced.

Lossless

Level of compression that has no discernable impact on the quality of the audio file, despite some data being discarded during the encoding process.

MB

Megabyte: one million bytes, where one byte is a single character, such as the letter 'a'. Used to measure the capacity of a device, such as the iPad, an iPod or a USB memory key. See also GB (gigabyte).

MobileMe

Online service run by Apple to provide a range of features of use to Mac and PC owners, including email, online storage, calendar synchronisation across multiple machines and basic backup tools (*left*). It is currently being phased out and replaced by iCloud. It is therefore not possible for new users to sign up to a MobileMe account, although those who were members before the introduction of iCloud have had their accounts extended.

MP3

Dominant form of audio compression, and the name that people give to files compressed in this way. Unpopular among many recording industry executives as it is difficult to impose copyright restriction measures on this format. This is the most common format for podcasts, and can be played by the iPad, iPhone and iPod.

Multitouch

Name given to Apple's technology for implementing on-screen actions by moving fingers around a seemingly inflexible display, such as that found on the iPad, iPhone (*below*) and iPod touch.

MacBook Air

Photo Stream

Synchronisation feature that is core to iOS 5, which backs up your last 1000 photos taken over the previous 30 days and synchronises them across all of your iOS-based devices. After 30 days they disappear from the stream, but so long as you update your iPhoto library at some point during that time they'll be backed up on your Mac (*above*).

Playlist

List of tracks drawn from one or more albums that will be played either in sequence or a random order, or burned to disc through the iTunes interface. Playlists can be copied between iTunes and the iPad, allowing you to take 'virtual' albums on the move.

Podcast

Non-live radio style broadcast downloaded through the iTunes podcast directory in the Music Store. Quality is highly variable. However, the likes of the BBC and Penguin Books have long seen the benefit of podcasting, which means a wide range of high quality material is now available for free.

Push email

Technology by which emails are sent from the server that holds them to a client device, such as a mobile phone or iPad, without you having to manually instigate a retrieval.

Rip

To extract audio from a CD for digital playback from a computer, or a portable device such as the iPad.

Sync

Contraction of *sync*hronise. To copy data from iTunes to an iPad, and pass data back to the computer, so that each device holds the same data.

USB 2.0

Hi speed connection method used to link iPads and either PCs or Macs. This replaced the FireWire cables used to connect older iPods and many video cameras, serving to make them more universally compatible.

Wifi

Once colloquial, but now generally-accepted term for wireless networking. It embodies several standards, of which the four most common are 802.11a, 802.11b, 802.11g and 802.11n. The 802.11a and 802.11g standards can each achieve a peak throughput of 54megabits/second. 802.11b runs at 11megabits/second, and 802.11n at 248megabits/second.

Wireless Access Point

Device that connects your network or broadband connection to your iPad and other computers.